## ST. LOUIS POST-DISPATCH

## BUSCH STADIUM   THE FIRST SEASON

### FIRST 500 PRINTED

This is to certify that this copy of the book

was No. **240** of the first 500 copies

of the first edition to print.

Kevin D. Mowbray, Publisher, St. Louis Post-Dispatch

ST. LOUIS POST-DISPATCH

# BUSCH STADIUM

# THE FIRST SEASON

# BUSCH STADIUM
# THE FIRST SEASON

**Editor**
Mike Smith

**Art Direction / Design**
Wade Wilson

**Photo Editor**
Larry Coyne

**Photographers**
Chris Lee and Post-Dispatch staff

**Contributing writers**
Joe Strauss, Derrick Goold, Bernie Miklasz,
Bill Smith, Bryan Burwell, Rick Hummel

**Assistant photo editor**
Hillary Levin

**Production coordinator**
Bob Rose

**Sales and marketing**
Gail LaFata, Nancy Long

Special thanks to Doug Weaver
of Kansas City Star Books

ISBN — 0-9661397-4-7
ISBN — 978-0-9661397-4-7

Printed by Walsworth Publishing Co., Marceline, Mo.

To order additional copies, call 800-329-0224.
Order online at www.post-dispatchstore.com

**RIGHT:** The Stan Musial statue,
transplanted from old Busch, remains
a drawing card at the new stadium.

**FAR RIGHT:** The Cardinals' first season
in their new ballpark ends with a rally
to celebrate their 2006 World Series title.

# CONTENTS

5

In January 2004, spray paint temporarily marks the spot for Busch Stadium's home plate.

In January 2005, new Busch Stadium is rising south of the stadium that has stood since 1966.

In December 2005, Busch Stadium absorbs its final blows from the wrecking ball.

By March 2006, old Busch is but a memory as new Busch nears completion.

Nostalgia buffs can still take the old concrete walkway across Eighth Street to get to new Busch Stadium.

Just like the old ballpark: Autograph hounds jockey for position along the railings at new Busch.

Every game of the first season at new Busch is a sellout, but Albert Pujols scores one of the best seats in the house while he waits to come off the disabled list.

On the ballpark's middle level, the Redbird Club is decorated with portraits of players from the early 1900s and is a popular gathering spot for fans.

## FROM "OUR BUSCH" TO NEW BUSCH   By Bill Smith

To stand here for a moment, high above the first base dugout as a strong spring wind whips through downtown, is to see a place at the very beginning of its life.

To my left, rows of scarlet seats stretch toward home plate, empty and waiting. To my right, still more seats bend toward the giant red letters that spell out "Budweiser" and the black video screen that rises blank and cold in right center field.

For now, at least, there is nothing to spoil the newness — not a single soft drink stain outlined on the concrete steps, not one stray peanut shell missed by the cleaning crew from the night before.

Sometime after 6 p.m. April 4, the gods of baseball willing, downtown's newest field of dreams will open for a minor-league game, in what city officials and area sports faithful hope will be a long and eventful run. Six days later, the park will host its first major-league game, between the Cardinals and the Milwaukee Brewers.

And while fans will cheer their flesh-and-blood heroes — Pujols, Carpenter, Rolen, Edmonds, Eckstein — much of the early attention will be riveted on a $365 million rookie performing before the home crowd for the first time.

To be honest, I never intended to like this place. I'd made up my mind months ago, even before we began scrawling our good-byes on the yellow foul poles of the old park and long before we watched the headache ball come crashing through the concrete rim of our Busch.

Our Busch served us for four decades and admittedly, in recent years, had begun to show her age. But she was clean, serviceable and the beer was always cold.

She may have been a concrete birthday cake, but she was our birthday cake. Besides, she had class, and history: Lou, Gibby, Gussie, Ozzie, '67, '82.

Then, just like that, she was gone. And suddenly, there was this:

something different, fancier, and, they told us, better.

It grew bigger and bigger until it overwhelmed the southern edge of downtown.

Somewhat grudgingly, I first visited the new park two days after Valentine's Day in a warm February rain. Several of us toured the clubhouse and the party rooms, remarking at the size and plushness of the suites and taking snapshots of the field that still stretched brown and grassless.

It was nice, nicer than I had thought. Still, I felt the pinch at my heart as I stood beyond the left field wall and looked at the graveyard where pieces of old Busch, our Busch, lay buried.

It was a month later before I returned and, when I did, I could feel the surge of energy and anticipation as hammers clattered and power saws screamed somewhere behind the drywall and wood.

This, I thought, could actually work. This, in fact, might be something good.

If old Busch was an enormous concrete cake, the new Busch seems like a giant, intricately planned Erector Set of red brick and black steel.

If the walkways of old Busch were dark and narrow, there is an exhilarating openness to the new park. It is a structure, in fact, almost extravagant in its openness, with open-air courtyards just behind the upper decks offering high-rise views of downtown.

Stand there and look across Broadway at the Mississippi River and the Arch. Stand here and look down on the morning traffic zipping along the Highway 40 overpass, not 30 yards away.

Some of the changes are enormous and bold: the giant black grandstand roofs reminiscent of yesterday's Sportsman's Park, the decidedly old-fashioned centerfield clock that replaces old Busch's digital timepiece, the massive open section in left centerfield that shows off the green-domed Old Courthouse and a wide swath of downtown.

Three weeks before the opener, Bud Chapall of Berlin, N.J., starts the decorative painting above the visitors dugout.

Some of the changes have been smaller: the little silver baseballs on the backs of each flip-down chair, each baseball marked with a seat number, and the carvings of baseballs and cardinals set into the brickwork of the backstop and the outside walls. The carvings bring a sense of history to a place with no history of its own.

And there is something else too, something so completely public and so intensely private — hundreds of bricks set into the ground and imprinted with names and dates and stories.

"Happy 50th, Darrell Davis," says one of the bricks, already positioned into the walkway outside the park.

"Jason W. Laramie," reads another, "Our Angel in the Outfield."

"The Best Father, Husband and Cardinals Fan. Thomas Lilley."

It is not perfect; nothing ever is. There are areas where low ceilings bring on a sense of claustrophobia. Ticket prices for special rooms seem unusually steep, especially in light of the scarcity of regular-seat tickets. It's a shame, too, that the old manual scoreboard could not have operated inside the current stadium, instead of being relegated to memento status and buffer to Highway 40.

But to see it all now and to sense the coming curtain-raising is to ask why I felt so overwhelmed by skepticism in the months as it was going up.

**16**

Historic views of the Cardinals logo adorn the brickwork at the new Busch Stadium.

Cardinals pitchers (from left) Mark Mulder, Jason Marquis, Braden Looper and Adam Wainwright check out the view from the pitcher's mound during a walk-through at the new stadium April 2. It's the team's first and only visit before the start of the season.

The answer, probably, is in the loyalty of the human spirit, the way we embrace things old and comfortable. For many of us, old Busch was the only baseball home we had ever known.

We celebrated birthdays there, anniversaries, championships. We saw 19 strikeouts in a single game and 70 home runs in a single season. We saw Schoendienst and Boyer and Whitey manage there, Carlton and Forsch pitch from the white rubber, and Musial and Buck in their crimson jackets wave to the cheering throngs.

But now we are here, with the 2006 season and every other season still ahead, waiting, trying to sense how this place will feel with the lights and the scorecard vendors and the roar of the crowd.

Today, it is a building— grand and impressive, to be sure — but only a building.

By April 10, it will be a major-league ballpark. In time, she will have history.

What will we say about this place in 40 years, in 2046?

How many games are there to be won, how many players still to be born, how many memories yet to be made?

On this day in early spring, this remains a place at the very beginning of its life.

Here, in this house of red brick, time begins on April 4, 2006.

Before the season, John Barton of St. Louis seeks his family's name among the 18,000 commemorative bricks outside Busch. He says reading so many bricks almost makes him dizzy, "I'm persistent. I'll find it," Barton says. The team later sends letters to brick buyers, giving locations of their purchases.

Julie Heyen (left) of Chesterfield, Mo., and Teresa Kintz of Webster Groves, Mo., explore Busch Stadium during a minor-league exhibition game April 4. "It's breathtaking," Kintz says. "I'm like a kid in a candy store."

# New park, old feelings

**April 10-13, 2006**

## MOMENTS

"Let's Get It Started" might've been the perfect, most obvious piece of musical trifle to open up the Cardinals' first game at the new Busch Stadium. But maybe the obvious wasn't what those programming the music were going for at that point.

Instead of the Black Eyed Peas favorite, fans heard Buster Poindexter's '80s favorite, "Hot Hot Hot," which nabbed the honors of being the song to roll out after the "let's play ball" pronouncement and a rendition of "The Star-Spangled Banner" by the fans, whom the announcer described as "the world's largest and finest choir."

— **Post-Dispatch**

They came, all 41,936 of them, to see something new. There awaited the lazy slope of a spanking new ballpark, mostly brick and painted red with freshly laid bluegrass and scoreboards offering sharper colors with vivid signage. Old Busch lay as a fond memory behind left field, its remnants cleared months ago. But better than merely offering some package just out of the box, new Busch provided those who drew near some fondly familiar scenes. Stan The Man leaned on Lou. The Clydesdales and the convertibles did their thing around the warning track. Carp and Albert, Cy Young and MVP, threw out first pitches to Willie McGee and Gibby, one of six Hall of Famers on the field. Less than three hours later, the Cardinals and starting pitcher Mark Mulder had taken a 6-4 win . . . with Albert Pujols contributing the first Cardinals home run in new Busch, a 445-foot bullet to lead off the third inning. ■

Tom Lange, of Spanish Lake, Mo., wears his Cardinals spirit on his head for the Busch Stadium opener.

— **Post-Dispatch coverage of April 10 Cardinals-Brewers game**

**RIGHT:** The rededication of the Musial statue leaves Stan the Man feeling right at home at the Eighth Street entrance of the new stadium.

## MOMENTS

You know you're getting old when another Busch Stadium goes up and Stan Musial, the greatest Cardinal of them all, hasn't played in that one, either.

But he was there at Busch No. 3, and while not as spry as he was when he won those seven batting titles at Sportsman's Park/Busch Stadium No. 1, the 85-year-old Hall of Famer was in his usual good humor as the Cardinals rededicated his statue outside the park.

Albert Pujols gave a warm embrace to Musial, who has called Pujols the best righthanded hitter he has seen on a Cardinals team. Who is going to dispute anything Stan the Man says in that arena?

— **Baseball columnist Rick Hummel**

## MOMENTS

"It's gorgeous. I love the wide outfield view of the Arch and the buildings. There is so much more to see than at the old stadium. The scoreboard is wonderful."

**— Cardinals fan Kate Vallowe, McLeansboro, Ill.**

Eight-year-old Alyssa Harris waits for the gates to open April 10.

Hall of Famer Stan "The Man" Musial, 85, takes it easy in an opening-day ride around the playing field.

A meeting of the greats: MVPs Willie McGee and Albert Pujols (left) and Cy Young Award winners Bob Gibson and Chris Carpenter. Pujols and Carpenter throw out the ceremonial first pitches.

## MOMENTS

Inauguration Day, baseball style, arrived in downtown St. Louis complete with hand-shaking dignitaries, booming brass bands and 66-year-old John Tomazic in his favorite pin-encrusted scarlet cowboy hat.

The retired coal miner from Bulpitt, Ill., who was attending his 50th consecutive Cardinals opening day, offered a snap assessment of new Busch Stadium.

"I'm tickled to death," Tomazic said. "The way it looks, it sort of brings back some old memories."

Tomazic should know. He was just a teenager in 1957 when he attended the first of his string of opening day games at Sportsman's Park.

— Post-Dispatch

Who else but Albert Pujols to christen the stadium with the first Cardinals home run? Pujols traces the trajectory of his third-inning solo shot.

## MOMENTS

My first strong impression of the new stadium wasn't a sight, or even a sound. Immediately inside the gate, it hit me: the exact same concession-stand-onion aroma, permeating the air throughout the main concourse, as in old Busch. I always figured that scent had become chemically bonded into the concrete of the old place, but right out of (or into) the gate, there it was in the brand-new park.

— Joe Bonwich,
food and restaurant writer
for the Post-Dispatch

Adam Bundren, with radio in one hand and drink in another, joins John Hentrich in celebrating Pujols' homer. They spend about 12 hours online, in virtual waiting rooms, trying to secure tickets for the opener. Instead they end up sitting at the north end of the stadium, outside the park, listening to the game on a radio.

## MOMENTS

Bill Niemietz snagged Busch Stadium's first-ever foul ball — off the bat of Cardinals leadoff man David Eckstein — with the simplest of moves.

"Boom, boom, boom, and it went under the seat," said Niemietz, of Glen Carbon, Ill. "I picked it up. Give me five years, and I'll be talking about my diving catch."

— **Post-Dispatch**

The Cardinals find an unusual power source in their new digs. Mark Mulder watches the flight of his two-run homer in the seventh inning. Mulder also excels on the mound and picks up the historic first victory.

## MOMENTS

"If you didn't feel something, then you don't have a heartbeat."

— Cardinals manager Tony La Russa, on the opening-day crowd singing the national anthem a cappella.

That's a winner! Albert Pujols tags Milwaukee's Gabe Gross for the final out of the game as closer Jason Isringhausen backs him up.

# Going ... going ... gone!

April 14-16, 2006

**S**wing by swing, deck by deck, Albert Pujols used his last three plate appearances to provide the Cincinnati Reds and a sellout crowd an Easter Sunday tour of new Busch Stadium. Not only did Pujols make some history, he turned what might have ended as a deflating loss into a memorable 8-7 win for a team still seeking its bearings in a new season as well as its fresh digs. Pujols extended the most impressive start of his career with three home runs worth five RBIs against three pitchers. The first smacked so hard against the Casino Queen Party Porch it could be heard miles away in the press box. The second bore into the lower left-field seats. The last shot crashed eight rows deep into the third deck 441 feet away. It turned a 7-6 deficit into a complicated, inspired reversal. Pujols had the second three-homer day and sixth walk-off home run of his career. A crowd of 40,068 had a keepsake. Asked the pitch location on Pujols' game-winner, no-nonsense Reds manager Jerry Narron said flatly, "Upper deck." ■

— **Post-Dispatch coverage of April 16 Cardinals-Reds game**

## MOMENTS

"You're watching all this happen and you're asking what else is he going to do, hit another one? And that's exactly what he does."

— **Cardinals pitcher Mark Mulder, on Albert Pujols' three-homer game Easter Sunday**

While Tony La Russa keeps track of the action, Albert Pujols stretches before an April 15 at-bat.

**No. 1** • (RIGHT) Albert Pujols watches his first of three home runs leave the park in the fifth inning of the April 16 game against Cincinnati.

**No. 2** • Pujols launches his second homer of the game in the seventh inning. "Now, I'm seeing the ball pretty good," he said. "Hopefully I can keep seeing the ball for another 150 games."

**No. 3** • A two-run shot in the bottom of the ninth brings the Cardinals an 8-7 victory, brings the fans to their feet and brings Pujols' teammates to home plate to celebrate.

Center fielder Jim Edmonds commits an error as he is unable to corral the bounce of a ball hit by Cincinnati's Austin Kearns. Kearns later scores on Aaron Harang's single. and the Cards lose 1-0.

The frustration continues for Edmonds, who yells as he strikes out swinging with the bases loaded to end the eighth inning of the 1-0 loss.

## MOMENTS

The updated team and the new stadium are works in progress. Both entities look pretty good, and have great potential, but there are problems.

For one, new Busch is leaking. ... Several empty sunflower-seed buckets were visible in the home-team clubhouse, placed at strategic locations to catch water dripping from the ceiling.

The infield and outfield are in sturdy shape, however. We know this because after one night game, the Cardinals held an unscheduled promotion. Let's call it, "The Owners' Kids Run The Bases Night."

Fred Hanser's son, Tim Hanser, led a group of giddy friends to the field to romp the bases and practice their sliding.

— **From an April column by Bernie Miklasz**

# And now ... the Cubs

**April 21-23, 2006**

## MOMENTS

Fans began lining up in the middle of the night to take advantage of a new ticket promotion that offers the chance to see the team play at its new home for less than the cost of a large beer.

The deal is the Cardinals' answer to the early bird special. The first 125 fans outside the ticket window at 9 a.m. the morning of each game can purchase a voucher for a pair of tickets for $11.

The voucher holders returned to the stadium 10 hours later, opening with excitement the ticket envelopes given to them by gate attendants. Many of the fans got a pair of infield box seats that usually sell for more than $70.

**— Post-Dispatch**

The last time the Cardinals played the Chicago Cubs, they found the experience as satisfying as a cold shower. Friday night, the teams met in 12-day-old Busch Stadium rather than 92-year-old Wrigley Field. Differences were to be expected. Temperatures on a clear night hovered in the low 70s instead of punishing those attending with a 20-degree wind-chill factor.

The Cardinals jumped the Cubs' starting pitcher. The bullpen, the slow-starting outfield and, even better, the showers worked. Topping it all, the Redbirds avoided their first five-game losing streak against the Cubs in a decade with a 9-3 win before 41,379. "No difference at all," said Cardinals backup catcher Gary Bennett, "except about 50 degrees." Third baseman Scott Rolen said, "The shower went much better tonight." Plugging a career moment into a bust-out month, first baseman Albert Pujols put the Cardinals and starting pitcher Mark Mulder (3-0) ahead to stay with his 1,000th base hit: a two-run, first inning home run. Pujols' 1,000th hit came in his 3,003rd career at-bat, tying him with Colorado Rockies first baseman Todd Helton as the second fastest to the milestone among active players. ■

Britta Vantrease, from Zeigler, Ill., and her boyfriend, David Droy of Winnebago, Ill., attend the first Cardinals-Cubs game at the new Busch Stadium.

**— Post-Dispatch coverage of April 21 Cardinals-Cubs game**

Gina Bone, of St. Charles, is the 125th and last person to get a voucher for two seats to the Friday Cardinals-Cubs game. Just before the game, she finds out her two $5.50 tickets are in the field boxes in section 160. She celebrates her good luck with fellow St. Charles resident Mike Vollmer.

## MOMENTS

"I wrote on my card 'play of the game.' If that ball gets by the third baseman, it's a completely different game and there's a good chance that the Cubs win and we don't. Just to keep the ball in the infield was a heck of a play. To get an out on it, that's vintage Scott Rolen."

**— Cardinals manager Tony La Russa, on Scott Rolen's backhand play that snuffs a bases-loaded rally by the Cubs on April 22**

**ABOVE:** Aramis Ramirez takes a hop as he tries to beat a throw by Scott Rolen.  Ramirez is ruled out as only one run scores on the bases-loaded play.  **RIGHT:** Albert Pujols makes his 1,000th career hit a biggie – a two-run homer against the Cubs.

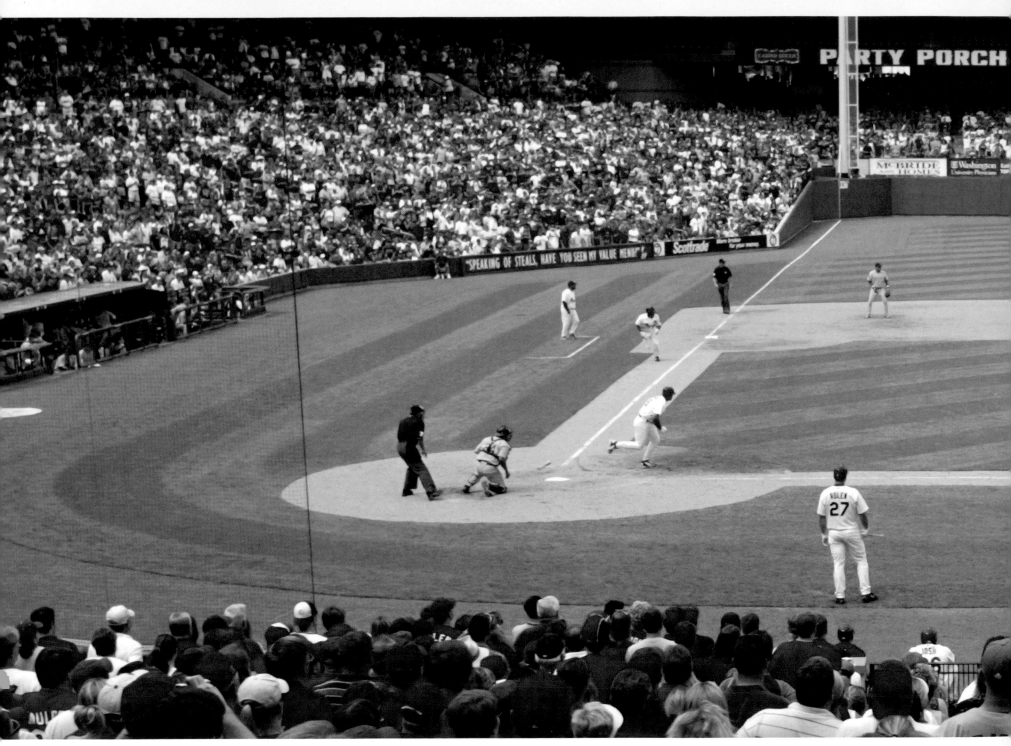

With the bases loaded, Albert Pujols pokes a two-run single off relief pitcher Scott Williamson past Chicago shortstop Ronny Cedeno for what turn out to be the game winning runs April 22.

## MOMENTS

"There's more excitement at the ballpark. It's special when you participate in something that has that kind of history and the fans are into it as much as they are.

"But winning the Cubs series won't be any more important than winning the one against the Pirates. You can't get fired up for one club you play five or six times a year and not get fired up for everybody you play. You won't get enough wins."

**— Tony La Russa,
on the Cards-Cubs rivalry**

Aaron Miles throws wide to first base after fielding a ball hit by Todd Walker. (FACING) Old master Greg Maddux and the Cubs have the Cardinals in control in the final game of the series.

# Coming around

**April 24-26, 2006**

## MOMENTS

Never one to shy from taking the extra base — in fact, it's in the DNA of his grit — Cardinals shortstop David Eckstein did something unusual in the ninth inning as he rounded second base. He stopped.

Having watched as the Pirates intentionally walked Albert Pujols twice previously, Eckstein chose not to take third on Hector Luna's single. To take third would have invited another walk for Pujols. So he put on the brakes. Pujols got to swing, and he drove in Eckstein with the winning run.

— Post-Dispatch story on David Eckstein setting the table for Albert Pujols to win the April 26 game

Earning bravos where once there were boos, Cardinals outfielder Juan Encarnacion led the rally of missing pieces with his clutch, his clout and his catch. Encarnacion's first home run of the season provided the difference and he drove in four runs, finishing a single short of the cycle in the Cardinals' 6-3 victory against Pittsburgh. A frosty 47 degrees greeted 38,809 in the chilliest game yet at Busch Stadium. The crowd, which had chirped at Encarnacion's struggles before this game, warmed with a standing ovation for his diving catch and commanded a curtain call for his pivotal two-out homer. "That shows you what Juan is capable of doing," manager Tony La Russa said. "We don't win that game without him being a hero, a star." Often this season, Encarnacion came up with a chance to ignite a big inning, only to fizzle. He'd manned the No. 2 spot more than any other Cardinal and gone stretches

High-fiving teammates await Juan Encarnacion after his two-run homer.

without delivering a key hit. Of his first 69 at-bats, 21 were with runners in scoring position and he'd managed to hit just .043. But this time he had three extra-base hits in his first three at-bats and drove in as many runs as he had in any game last season. ■

— Post-Dispatch coverage of April 25 Cardinals-Pirates game

David Eckstein slides safely into home plate as no throw is made to Pittsburgh catcher Ronny Paulino on a single by Scott Spiezio.

Juan Encarnacion makes a diving catch to rob Ronny Paulino of an extra-base hit.

Cardinals center fielder Jim Edmonds (left) calls out to right fielder Juan Encarnacion after Encarnacion's acrobatic catch.

## MOMENTS

His position is listed as center field, but within the Cardinals' clubhouse Jim Edmonds' home is The Corner, an unofficial sanctuary for veterans where outsiders tread at their own risk.

The Corner once belonged to Mark McGwire. Edmonds was deeded the space in old Busch Stadium in 2002, and the neighborhood has since housed graybeards Tino Martinez, Reggie Sanders, and Ray Lankford. Scott Rolen and Scott Spiezio now reside in his ZIP code.

"It's a different feeling without guys like Larry (Walker) and Reggie around," Edmonds said. "There are a lot of different faces here — a lot of good guys but there's been a lot of turnover. That's just the way the game is now. But to be here the whole time watching it is a little weird."

**— Post-Dispatch story on Jim Edmonds**

# Walking the line

**April 27-30, 2006**

## MOMENTS

A cardboard box ablaze on the mezzanine level of Busch Stadium's left-field stair tower caught the attention of the Cardinals' manager and television cameras and brought fire investigators to the new ballpark.

Cardinals manager Tony La Russa phoned the press box when he saw the fire from the dugout in the eighth inning. "I thought somebody was having a cookout," La Russa said, "but we don't allow that, do we?"

Cardinals players saw the fire from the field. "Put it out quick," third baseman Scott Spiezio said. "We just got this field. We don't want it to go up in smoke."

— **Post-Dispatch coverage of the April 27 game.**

"I hope they walk him 150 times this year." The speaker was Cardinals center fielder Jim Edmonds, and the subject was teammate Albert Pujols. And, after four consecutive walks for Pujols, including one intentional with runners already on first and second, he is on pace for 181 walks this season. But perhaps that pace will slow if Edmonds cleans up after Pujols. Edmonds, making the most of his 16 hits this season, drove in three runs with two singles — both coming after Pujols walks — as the Cardinals whipped Washington 9-2. Edmonds has 19 runs batted in, second to Pujols' 31, for the few hits he has had. He is batting .213. "So, I'm not so (awful), just a little (awful)," Edmonds joked. "I'm not totally worthless. I've worked on catching the ball now (he had two errors in one game in the first home stand), I've gotten a few RBIs. Now I've got to work on getting a few more hits. ... They can walk (Pujols) all year as far as I'm concerned. It's perfect for me. I get a chance to drive in some runs and show some people I can still play." ■

Jim Edmonds tries to pick up the pace ... and a few RBIs to make teams pay for walking Albert Pujols.

— **Post-Dispatch coverage of April 30 Cardinals-Nationals game**

Albert Pujols laughs as he looks down the third-base line to coach Jose Oquendo (far right) after Washington reliever Joey Eischen throws a wild pitch while trying to intentionally walk him .

Sidney Ponson hides under his hat after backing up home plate on a two-run double by Washington's Brian Schneider. (RIGHT) Ozzie Smith is tackled by Nationals special advisor Jose Cardenal as they greet each other during batting practice.

## MOMENTS

Ozzie Smith, 51, is finishing up a 10-year, $2 million personal services contract with the Cardinals that started upon his retirement in 1996, but most of the services have had little to do with anything on the field. His commitment has consisted mostly of being on hand for opening day festivities and before playoff and World Series games.

While Smith rarely is on the field anymore, he hasn't lost his interest in the game. But there are some things that bother him about baseball, such as the decline in the running game (Smith stole 580 bases).

"It's gone," Smith said. "We've adopted the American League philosophy."

— Post-Dispatch

# Stars shine

**May 8-10, 2006**

**MOMENTS**

*"He's a game changer. That's about as big a compliment as you can pay a player."*

**— Rockies manager Clint Hurdle, on Albert Pujols.**

While 2005 Cy Young Award winner Chris Carpenter wasn't rewarded with victory, his partner in hardware, 2005 Most Valuable Player Award winner Albert Pujols, made sure the Cardinals got the most out of the night's exercise. With two on and nobody out in the eighth inning and Jose Mesa pitching, Pujols drilled his 17th homer, giving the Cardinals — and Adam Wainwright — a 4-2 victory. While there would be no win for Carpenter, there would be win No. 1 in the big leagues for Wainwright. The spectacular Wainwright worked just one inning — a perfect one in the eighth — and then closer Jason Isringhausen allowed no further tremors, fanning the side in the ninth for his ninth save. "That's the 'Izzy' that I know," Pujols said. "That's the guy I know for the last three years." Wainwright, who has an earned-run average of 0.57, was appreciative of his good fortune. "'Carp' definitely deserves this win," Wainwright said. "But you also can give the win to Albert Pujols, too. The guy's a superstar who bails us out ... time in and time out ... every day." ◼

Chris Carpenter shows his frustration after an error helps Colorado tie the game.

**— Post-Dispatch coverage of May 9 Cardinals-Rockies game**

Albert Pujols waits in foul territory to catch a pop-up off the bat of Colorado's Matt Holliday.

## MOMENTS

"It's a pitcher's park. It's pretty tough. I've hit some balls to right field and center and Jimmy (Edmonds) has hit some balls ... it's amazing they are all staying in.

"But that's part of the game. There's nothing you can do. It's a nice stadium."

— Albert Pujols

**LEFT:** Jason Marquis tries to regroup after allowing a two-run single to Brad Hawpe. **ABOVE:** Matt Holliday is congratulated by teammates as he returns to the dugout after hitting his second solo homer on May 8.

## MOMENTS

"Our biggest question mark was the bullpen this year. And these young kids have been on my butt about pitching better. I don't like being shown up by people, especially these kids."

— Cards closer
Jason Isringhausen

LEFT: Rockies reliever Ray King prepares to face ex-teammate Jim Edmonds. ABOVE: Juan Encarnacion
makes a surprise visit to the box seats after snagging a foul fly by Colorado's Matt Holliday.

# Redbirds in the pink

**May 12-14, 2006**

There usually isn't a lot of pink in baseball clubhouses, but in Cardinals shortstop David Eckstein's locker sat two pink baseball bats.

The bats are Louisville Sluggers made to Eckstein's normal specifications, except that these bats have a breast cancer awareness ribbon printed on them, and under Eckstein's imprinted signature is not his name but that of his mother, Patricia. Oh, and they've been painted pink.

Eckstein is one of about 50 big leaguers who used a pink bat on Mother's Day; it was auctioned off to raise money for the Susan G. Komen Breast Cancer Foundation.

— Post-Dispatch

Albert Pujols again did something never done before. For Scott Rolen, it only seemed that way. On a night when Pujols reached 19 home runs faster than any player in the game's history, Rolen ended a stretch of 46 at-bats without an RBI by driving in five runs with a first-inning home run and a fourth-inning double. Coupled with Pujols' three RBIs and two hits from Jim Edmonds, the Cardinals' "MV3" rose again in a 9-1 pounding of the Arizona Diamondbacks. The breakout coincided with Jason Marquis' first win since April 17, a seven-inning, three-hit performance that gained speed after an uneasy opening. Rolen was slowed for almost two weeks by a viral condition that sapped his energy and about 10 pounds, and it took the Cardinals third baseman longer to get his next RBI than for Marquis to get his next win. "It probably seems longer to me than to you. I felt

Three Cardinals — David Eckstein, Jim Edmonds and Scott Spiezio — use pink bats during a Mother's Day game.

some guys on my back a little bit," said Rolen, who had waited since April 16 for his 14th RBI. The drought lasted long enough for some people to forget who he is; the stadium's video display referred to him as "Roland." ∎

— **Post-Dispatch coverage of  May 13 Cardinals-Diamondbacks game**

Juan Encarnacion (center) guides teammate Scott Rolen away from home plate as Rolen argues a called strikeout with umpire Marvin Hudson on May 12.

The Cardinals add their retired numbers to the left-field wall after the season starts. Fans had complained that the numbers are not prominently displayed behind the right-field bleachers, so the Cardinals add the left-field tribute.

## MOMENTS

"For the fans in St. Louis to be booing Encarnacion, I don't think that was right. You're booing him right now, but when he gets his approach, everybody's going to love him.

"The guy's really frustrated right now. He's trying to do as much as he can to help us win and the last thing you want is for our fans, 45,000 people, booing a guy like that. I don't think that's the right way to approach it."

**— Albert Pujols,**
**during Juan Encarnacion's**
**slow start to the '06 season**

Manager Tony La Russa pats right fielder Juan Encarnacion on the cheek after he replaces him during a game against the Diamondbacks.

Arizona third baseman Chad Tracy catches a pop foul to end John Rodriguez's at-bat during a drizzly game May 14.

Pujols had never homered more than 12 times or exceeded 29 RBIs in a month until now. He's hitting a homer every 5.7 at-bats after homering every 14.6 at-bats in his first five seasons. But he isn't shooting for the fences. Pujols' hitting discipline remains intact.

And so it was on his winning homer this day. Instead of trying to yank a homer down the left-field line, Pujols rifled a pitch 411 feet into the right-field bullpen.

"He may finish with 30 homers," manager Tony La Russa said. "His goal is to just get a good swing, and he doesn't deviate. So he's going to hit line drives. And when he clicks it, the ball can go out of the ballpark. He's just playing the game the way he always does, giving us our best chance to win. It could be singles or doubles — but in April, 2006 it's home runs."

St. Louis hasn't witnessed this kind of power surge since Mark McGwire's summer of 1998. But Pujols isn't trying to wreck any home run records.

"The job is to go out there with a good approach, get a good pitch to hit, and get a good swing," Pujols said. "Try for your best swing, and if the ball goes out of the park, so what? If it doesn't, so what? The key is to try and get on base, and contribute to try and win the game."

Pujols saved three errors in this game, retrieving two scattered throws by third baseman Scott Spiezio. After Isringhausen walked the bases loaded with two outs in

Albert Pujols sets a major-league record for most home runs (14) in April.

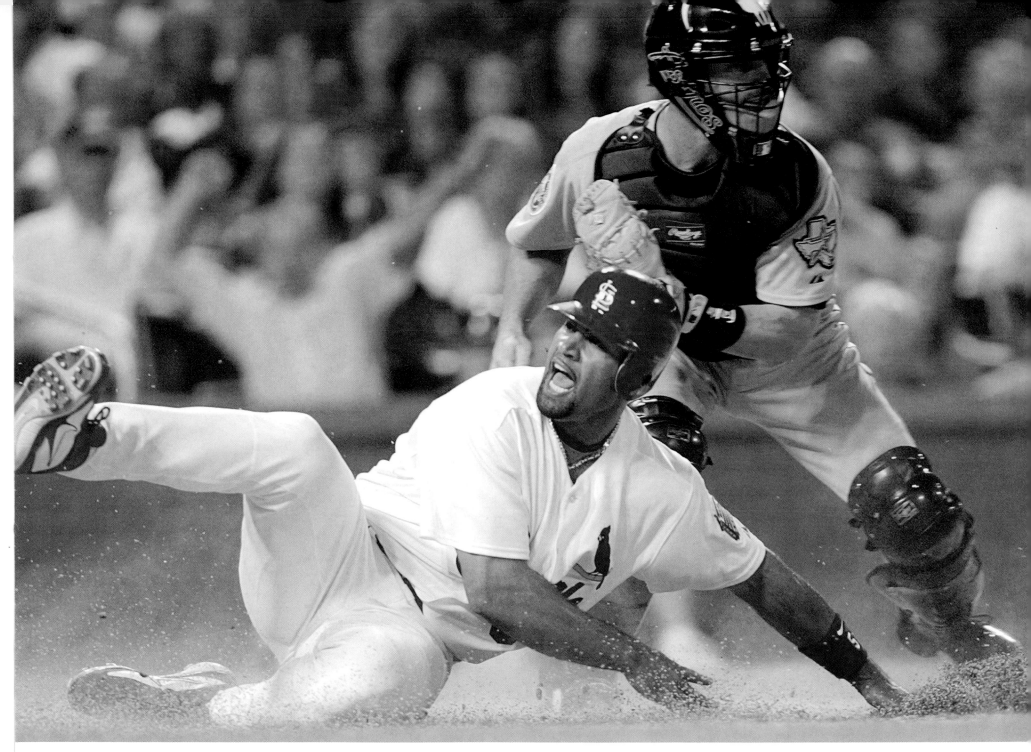

Baserunning is one of Pujols' strengths, but Astros catcher Brad Ausmus nails him at home when Pujols tries to score on a grounder to third in the May 30 game.

# 'Win the series'

**May 16-18, 2006**

A charming new detail has been added to the outfield wall: graphic images and bold block numbers of all the retired jerseys of Cardinals legends.

The images carry the weight of history and the pure romance of St. Louis' most beloved boys of summer. Yet there is a name, a face and a number that seems to be missing: No. 51, Willie McGee.

McGee's career probably falls just shy of Hall of Fame consideration. But this isn't about pure stats. This is about pure love and affection, and sometimes that means a lot more.

— **May 16 column by Bryan Burwell**

A s if born to write bumper stickers, Cardinals manager Tony La Russa has a trusty collection of catchy phrases he likes to trot out sometimes as answers, sometimes as shields. It may not have the marketability of "Play a Hard 9," the insight of "tied for first," or the wit of "men not machines," but another pet motto starred in this game:

"Win the series."

Riding a second consecutive solid start by Jason Marquis, three hits by leadoff hitter David Eckstein and two RBIs by fill-in first baseman Scott Spiezio, the Cardinals claimed the series of division leaders with a 6-3 victory against the New York Mets. The Cardinals have won all eight series they have played at Busch Stadium.

A 1-0 victory over the Mets rubs Mark Mulder, Yadier Molina and Albert Pujols the right way.

Five times this season, the Cardinals needed to win the third of three games to claim a series. All five times, they have won, with Jason Isringhausen closing his third straight rubber game.

"I'm going to pretend I didn't hear that," said La Russa, quickly employing another favorite tic: thumping wood. "I much prefer winning the first two and then we go for the gusto in the third. ... The goal is to win the series.

"Just win the series." ■

— **Post-Dispatch coverage of May 18 Cardinals-Mets game**

Hector Luna scores past Mets catcher Paul Lo Duca on a sacrifice fly by David Eckstein. Luna's versatility and speed help the Cardinals early in the season.

The series opener leaves the Cardinals slipping. **ABOVE:** Jim Edmonds drops his bat and helmet at home plate after striking out to end the fourth inning.
**FACING:** Trainer Greg Hauck, catcher Gary Bennett and Tony La Russa attend to Albert Pujols after he slips on a wet field while  tracking a foul pop.

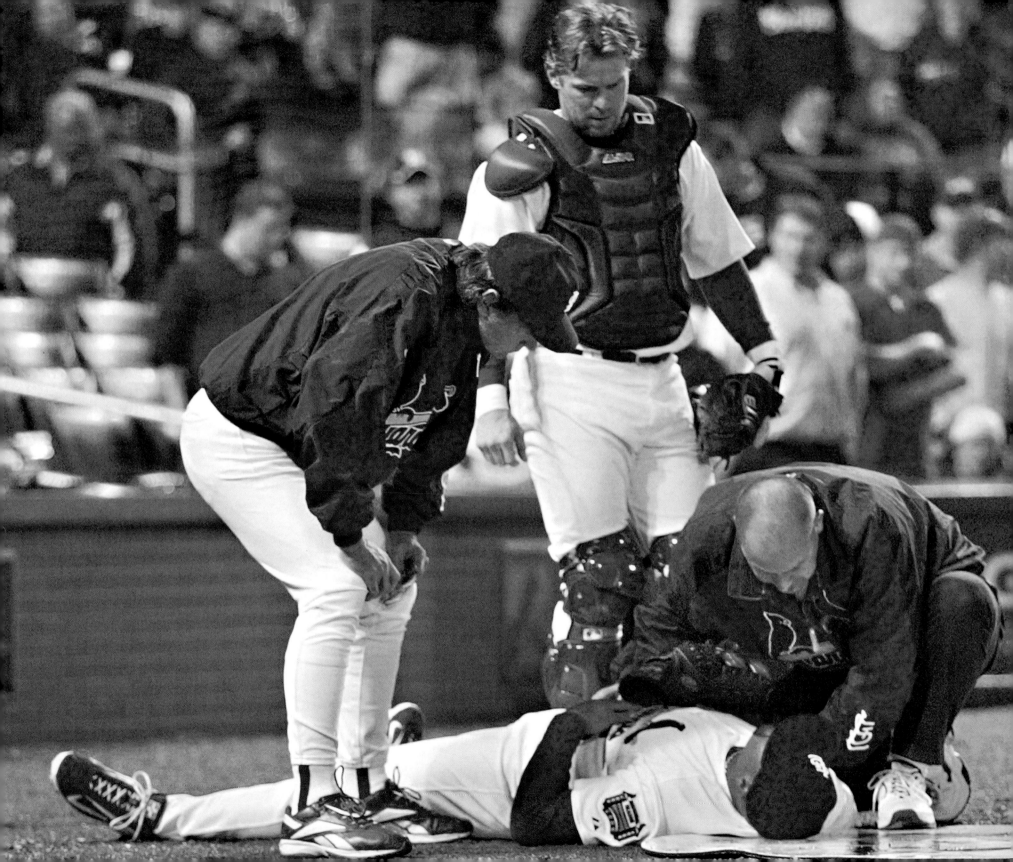

# A full house pays off

**May 29-31, 2006**

In the same situation with the same score two innings earlier, Albert Pujols had struck out, the rarest feat of all for him this season. But given a second chance, Pujols did what even his teammates have come to expect from him during this pyrotechnic season.

He gave the folks sitting in the newly opened left field seats a view of what they've missed so far this season.

Pujols launched a two-out, three-run homer in the seventh inning to upend Houston's one-run lead and win the game for the Cardinals 3-1. A burr for the Cardinals suits this season has been that the replays of so many of his history-making homers have featured an expanse of empty seats because 4,176 seats remained unopened until Memorial Day.

As if playing to the new house - full for the first time - Pujols' 25th home run soared high, arcing at the height of the new seats. Replays will have a nice pan of the packed place.

"Hottest man on the planet with somebody in scoring position," Houston manager Phil Garner said. "At first, it looked like it wasn't going to go out and then I think the God of baseball grabbed it and pushed it out." ■

— Post-Dispatch coverage of May 29 Cardinals-Astros game

## MOMENTS

"It looks a little better with people in those seats, doesn't it? You'd see the highlights and balls would be hit into empty seats. I don't know how many calls I got from people who said, 'Hey, I thought you were sold out.'"

— Cardinals vice president of ticket sales Joe Strohm, after the May 29 opening of 4,000-plus seats in left field

Roy Oswalt, who started the last game at old Busch Stadium, starts the first game with a full crowd at new Busch Stadium.

Busch Stadium's full capacity of 43,975 is achieved when the left-field seats are opened for the first time during a Memorial Day game against Houston.

David Eckstein is hit on the wrist by a pitch in the bottom of the 11th inning May 31. That loads the bases for So Taguchi, who delivers the game-winning hit.

For Albert Pujols, very few moments around the game are wasted. He takes some practice swings by the bat rack in the dugout.

## MOMENTS

So Taguchi became the hub for The Bounce, a team celebration of Taguchi's two-out, bases loaded single that beat the Houston Astros 4-3 in 11 innings.

Taguchi then carried out the ceremonial part when he folded his hands and bowed to his ecstatic manager, Tony La Russa.

"I can't be Jimmy," said Taguchi, who replaced the injured Jim Edmonds. "I can't hit home runs like him. I can't make the same catches. But I can go out there and play to my best."

**— Post-Dispatch coverage of the May 31 game**

Yadier Molina celebrates with teammate Albert Pujols after Molina comes across the plate with the winning run in the bottom of the 11th inning

So Taguchi gets a hug from teammate John Rodriguez after driving in the winning run. Taguchi's single pushes the Cardinals to 15 games over .500 and makes them a perfect nine for nine in winning series at home.

# A pain in the side

**June 2-4, 2006**

They won 100 games last season despite rarely playing whole. Now, with their run-producing machine barely able to breathe without wincing, the Cardinals offered some of the same by recovering from a day-old injury and a pitcher's difficult start to overtake the Chicago Cubs 9-6.

With first baseman Albert Pujols going on the disabled list, the Cardinals reclaimed Gold Glove center fielder Jim Edmonds from an abdominal strain and placed him at Pujols' vacated position.  The NL Central leaders' reward was a nine-hit pounding of Cubs starter Greg Maddux.

"This is who we are. This is how we play," manager Tony La Russa said. "You play with who you have. The expectations are the same. That part never changes."

If not for Pujols' injury, Edmonds might have been the one to land on the disabled list. Instead, Edmonds contributed three hits and two RBIs.

Cubs slugger Derrek Lee (broken wrist) spends the weekend in the dugout.

"Tony and I talked yesterday about whether I thought I was going on the DL or not," Edmonds said. "He wanted to know would I be ready or was I shutting it down? I told him I was ready to play three days ago but it wasn't possible. It worked out well." ■

**— Post-Dispatch coverage of June 4 Cardinals-Cubs game**

Albert Pujols tries to work out the kinks after moving too quickly to run down a pop foul. After consulting with Tony La Russa and Greg Hauck, Pujols completes the inning, but not the June 3 game. He says he felt a "pop" in his side. The diagnosis: a torn right oblique and a trip to the disabled list.

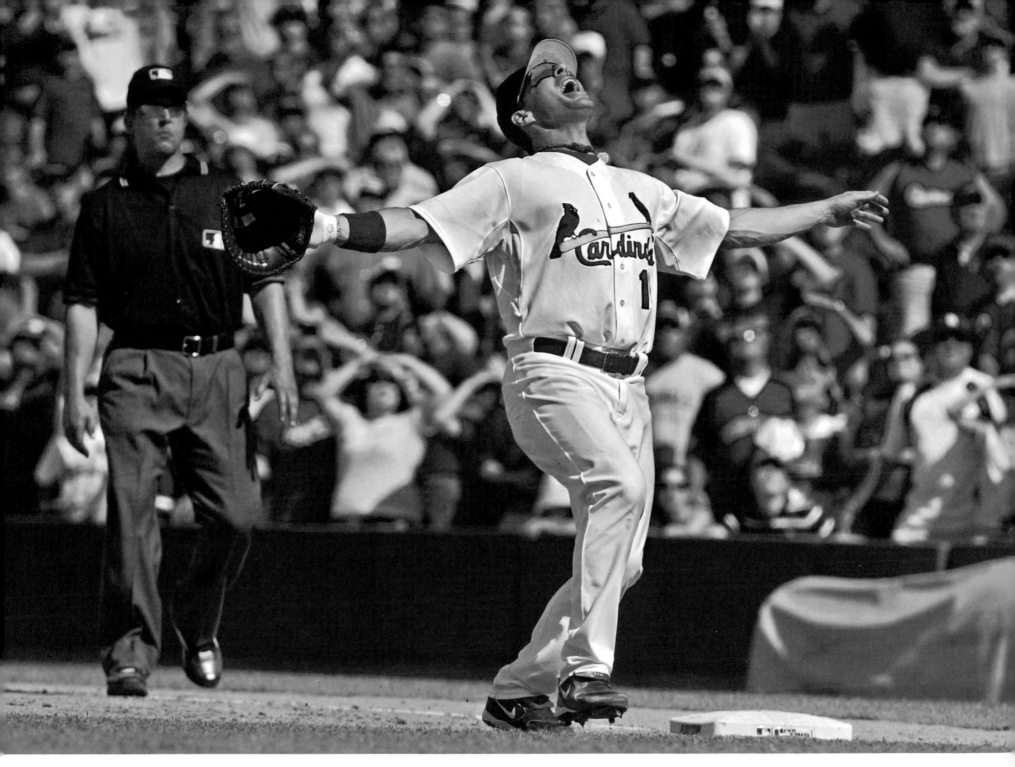

Jim Edmonds corrals a pop fly hit by Chicago's Phil Nevin. Edmonds seems ticketed for the disabled list until Albert Pujols goes down. The Gold Glove center fielder is called on to play first base, and he does so flawlessly.

## MOMENTS

Beyond the walls of the brickyard on Broadway, there is panic in the streets. You can hear the shrill voices of dread and the high-pitched wails of gloom and doom. These are the primal shrieks of Cardinal Nation in frothing anguish and sweaty despair, because the best little baseball town in America woke up to the cataclysmic headlines that their larger-than-life folk hero was injured.

The news of Albert Pujols' sudden demise was made even more alarming by the uncomfortable truth that nobody really knows exactly what an oblique muscle is. All you know is that the irreplaceable Prince Albert could be out of action for as long as six weeks, and that's enough bad news to scare legions of Redbirds fanatics into full-blown anxiety.

— Columnist Bryan Burwell

Pete Tanzillo of Kewanee, Ill., helps 18-month-old grandson Maddux Dasenbrook of Baltimore touch home plate at Busch Stadium during a "Run The Bases Day" promotion June 4.

# Storm amid the calm

**June 5-7, 2006**

These are strange times in America's best baseball town. Other than understandably venting some frustration, the fans are reasonably calm. But inside the Cardinals fraternity, the environment is stressed. Many grumps. A quiet clubhouse. Long faces. Granted, no one should be happy after losses. But it's more than that.

## MOMENTS

*"Albert's injury was a tough break, missing Jimmy was a tough break, but it wasn't like anybody felt sorry for us.*

*"But it's not like we're under some black cloud, because here comes Chris. Here comes Chris."*

**— Tony La Russa, as Cy Young Award winner Chris Carpenter returned from the disabled list June 6**

The grim, almost desperate vibe around this ballclub is unsettling. We haven't seen this type of sourness with a Cardinals team since 2003, when the atmosphere turned toxic down the stretch.

And there was no relief as the emboldened Reds cranked out a 7-4 win to complete a three-game sweep and move into a first-place tie with St. Louis in the NL Central. This team has been a bully in the past two seasons, so it is surprising to see the Cardinals getting slapped around in the division.

Former Cardinal Esteban Yan jokingly looks for Cardinals' Albert Pujols' strained oblique muscle.

"We had a really rough series," manager Tony La Russa said. "And they had a very good series. They did a lot of things right." ∎

**— Post-Dispatch coverage of June 7 Cardinals-Reds game**

Closer Jason Isringhausen waits on the mound to be relieved by manager Tony La Russa after allowing a go-ahead three-run homer to Cincinnati's Ken Griffey Jr. in the ninth on June 5.

## MOMENTS

"When you're working with people on base every night it gets pretty frustrating. Frustrating for me. Frustrating for the guys on the team. Frustrating for the fans. Frustrating for everybody."

— **Cards closer
Jason Isringhausen**

## MOMENTS

"I always felt I had to prove I was worthy. Especially being a first-round pick and having your dad as a coach. I don't want anything ever to be just handed to me, and that perception was something hard for me to deal with at first.

"The more success I've had, the more comfortable I am with it all. Whereas before, if I had a bad year, people were looking at me and didn't take me seriously."

**— Rookie slugger Chris Duncan, son of pitching coach Dave Duncan**

Pinch-hitter Chris Duncan acknowledges the crowd's request for a curtain call after hitting a two-run homer against the Reds on June 5.

## MOMENTS

There probably will be lots of debate and speculation about who might be available and who might be given up in a trade to compensate for the loss of Albert Pujols. But the most important component in the Cardinals' season is not in the batting order, it's on the mound. The key to surviving the injury to Pujols or an injury to any everyday player is the performance of the pitching staff.

That is the strength of the club, the element that will sustain it, the foundation for a postseason appearance or a fall from contention. To tinker with that component is risky business. It has a rhythm, karma, a life of its own. Removing and adding pieces, even when they are considered of equal or greater value, can taint the mix.

— **Columnist Dan O'Neill**

The dugouts are scenes of jubilation and frustration. Tony La Russa (facing) mulls a ninth-inning Ken Griffey homer. Reds pitcher Aaron Harang shows a different reaction to a Cardinals three-run outburst.

# Comforts of home

**June 16-18, 2006**

S ome Cardinals have taken longer than others to familiarize themselves with their new ball-park. In less than three months, right fielder Juan Encarnacion has discovered the entrance and the exit to Busch Stadium's lost and found.

A minimal presence in April, Encarnacion continued his recent offensive flex with two home runs and a late double in the Cardinals' 6-5 win over the Colorado Rockies. A verbal pincushion for fan discontent in the season's opening weeks, Encarnacion rode a wave of applause from 45,968, the largest crowd to watch a game in new Busch.

Encarnacion's three-hit breakout helped starting pitcher Jeff Suppan to his 100th career win in exchange for 7 ⅔ solid innings, and the Cardinals to their seventh win in 12 games without disabled first baseman Albert Pujols.

Tony La Russa congratulates starting pitcher Jason Marquis for a solid eight-inning effort against the Rockies on June 16.

No longer the jumpy hitter who struck out 17 times in April before finding his second RBI in his new team's 19th game, Encarnacion took the night in typically languid stride.

"It's like I've said before: My numbers are going to be there at the end of the season. It's not how you start; it's how you finish," he said. "It takes awhile to get to know your way around. Now I feel more comfortable with everybody and myself." ■

— **Post-Dispatch coverage of June 17 Cardinals-Rockies game**

## MOMENTS

"The carry here is fair. You've still got to hit it, but the balls down the lines carry a little bit better here than in the old park. But the ball doesn't carry toward the bullpens, where the solid wall is in front of the bleachers."

— Cardinals coach
Jose Oquendo,
upon learning
that home runs
were up 16 percent at
new Busch Stadium

Juan Encarnacion makes fans forget about his slow start to the season after hitting two homers and a double on June 17.

The new stadium allows fans to get closer to the action, and to their favorite Cardinals for autographs before the game.

Angel accompanies her owner, Rick Eiken of Jefferson City, Mo., to the June 18 game at Busch Stadium as part of the "Pooches at the Park" event. The back of Angel's jersey reads "Poochols."

# By the seat of their pants

**June 26-28, 2006**

At around 10:20 p.m., there were UFO sightings at Busch Stadium. Little flying saucers, hundreds of them, began landing on the infield, the outfield, the warning track, and the dugouts. And a ballgame suddenly turned into a scene from a Spielberg film.

A closer look revealed that the UFOs were actually white seat cushions, hurled out of the stands, spinning like Frisbees, sent skyward by delirious fans who celebrated the end of an eight-game losing streak the way some heralded VJ Day, or Lindbergh's arrival in Paris.

The flying objects were a bit much, yes. But St. Louis is, after all, a berserk baseball town. And it is a baseball town that does not fancy losing. And it is a baseball town that was in an especially foul mood earlier, hissing and booing reliever Jason Isringhausen as the bullpen frittered away a 3-1 lead — mostly due to inept fielding — in Cleveland's three-run eighth.

Cardinals fans aren't used to sitting on their fannies, or their seat cushions, watching the local nine stumble and fumble through games, doing a disturbing impersonation of the Kansas City Royals.

So when the Cardinals took advantage of two klutzy Cleveland errors in the bottom of the ninth to score two runs, claim a 5-4 win on Seat Cushion Night and terminate the dreaded streak, the eruption was predictable, if over the top. ∎

**— Post-Dispatch coverage of June 28 Cardinals-Indians game**

## MOMENTS

*"I don't think this team is going to be down too much longer. Once we get that little click it's going to be scary what this team is going to do."*

**— Rookie pitcher Anthony Reyes, on June 27 after the Cardinals' losing streak reaches eight, the franchise's longest since 1988**

Ronnie Belliard, then an Indian, later a Cardinal, is plunked by Jason Marquis on June 26.

Juan Encarnacion normally doesn't show much emotion, but an eight-game losing streak will do this to a ballplayer.

## MOMENTS

His office is bedecked with a couple flat-screen TVs and a laptop computer that's more a prop than a tool. If he wanted more high-tech touches for his home at Busch Stadium, there's no doubt manager Tony La Russa would get hooked up, dialed in and logged on.

But he won't find the universal remote he seeks. There's no way he can zap what happened this past week against AL Central teams.

"I was looking forward to good competition," the Cardinals skipper said. "However you want to come in and explain it or excuse it, the competition had been, well ... There was no competition.

"And that's real irritating. We're better than we showed. I believe that. If I could, I would find a way and rewind what happened and play the games again."

**— From a story headlined "Redbirds are humbled by whipping from AL Central"**

98

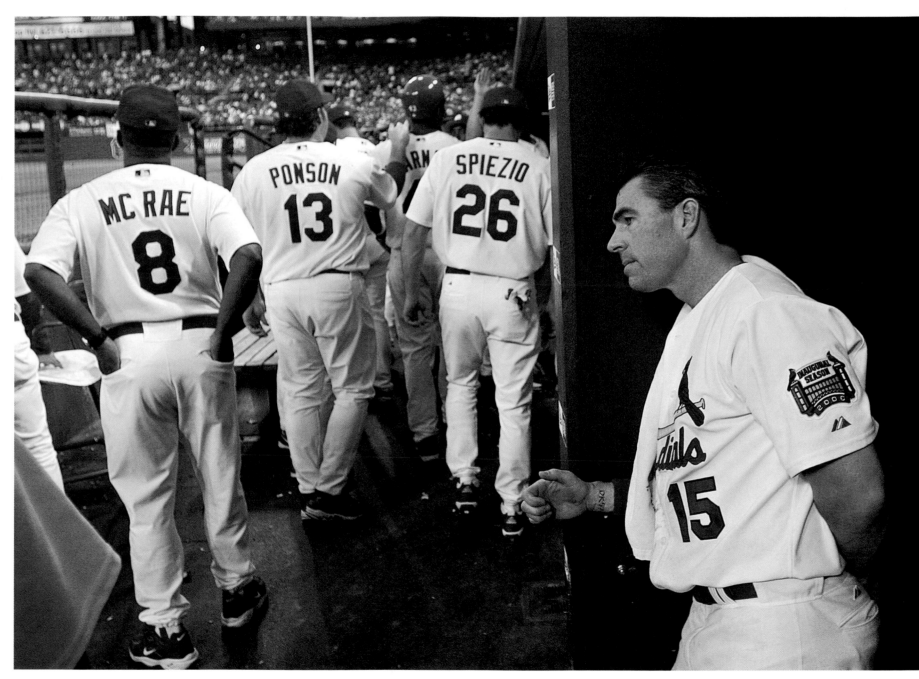

**FACING:** Cleveland outfielder Grady Sizemore goes airborne in an attempt to rob Hector Luna of a double. **ABOVE:** Jim Edmonds reflects on his baserunning gaffe. Teammate Juan Encarnacion scores on the play, but Edmonds is out rounding third.

The streak is over. Albert Pujols hops the dugout rail to be the first on the field to celebrate as the Cardinals snap their losing streak on an error in the bottom of the ninth.

Seat cushions litter the field after fans throw them from the seats to celebrate the end of the eight-game losing streak on June 28.

La Russa is crazy or brilliant or a combination of both. I have to 'fess up and admit that when I first heard Edmonds was in the lineup, I thought La Russa had cracked under the strain of losing games to rival Dusty Baker.

Didn't La Russa learn anything from last summer, by writing Scott Rolen into the lineup with a damaged shoulder that later would require a second, major operation?

As it turns out, La Russa was operating on presumably responsible medical advice. So we extend our apologies for thinking scurrilous thoughts … unless, of course, Edmonds' abdominal wall collapses. And then all recantations are off.

For those of us ignorant of sports medicine it does seem odd to think that it was normal for Edmonds to play a full-scale game less than two days after pinch hitting was deemed too hazardous to his health.

"There's no way he would have played if there was any kind of risk of significant damage," La Russa said. "That would have been stupid. It's the beginning of June. It was explained to me

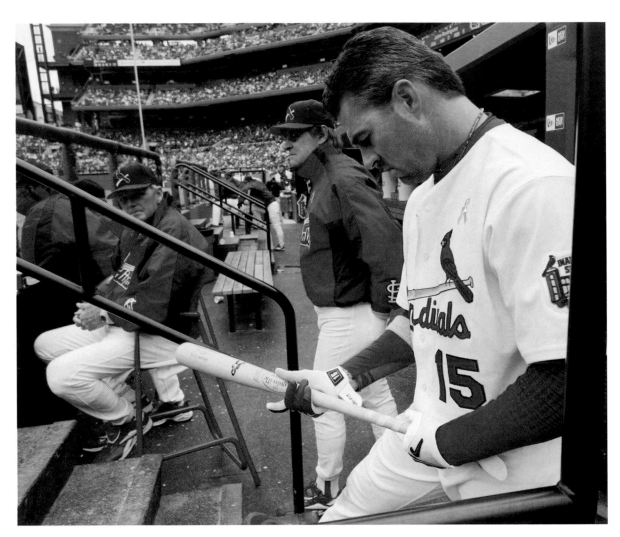

Jim Edmonds uses a pink bat on Mother's Day, and the bat is auctioned off after the game to raise money for charity.

Jim Edmonds looks out of place, hanging with pitchers (from left) Jeff Suppan, Jason Isringhausen, Chris Carpenter and Jeff Weaver during batting practice Aug. 29.

that this was an injury that will not get worse. It may get more sore, but it will not get worse."

The hope is that this won't deteriorate into Rolen II. And this wasn't a hasty call. La Russa had lengthy discussions with the medical staff, general manager Walt Jocketty and Edmonds. All parties were on board with the decision. But then again, the team framed the storyline the same way with Rolen last summer.

I asked Edmonds if he feared catastrophe by playing at less than 100 percent.

"Am I worried about it? No. Have I thought about it? A little bit," he said. "But I feel I can control myself enough in being at first, and being in control of my running around the bases, that I can limit what the effort is. And hopefully I won't put myself at risk."

This will be an interesting, anxious time. Fans will hold their breath when Edmonds makes a sudden move. And if Edmonds comes through this without a mishap, no one will exhale more strenuously than Manager La Russa.

Edmonds does an adequate job as a fill-in first baseman, but he's still one of baseball's best at tracking flies in center.

Teammates salute Edmonds after he ties a game against the Dodgers with a home run.

# Hammers at the heart

**June 30 - July 2, 2006**

**MOMENTS**

I realize that we love small ball in St. Louis. It's considered pure and old-school and cerebral. But few modern teams are equipped to win in this manner.

To win in 2006, you'd better have clout. Compared to last season, the home-run rates are on the rise around Major League Baseball. ... Steals and bunts are nice accessories, but this is still a game for the boppers and bammers.

Muscle is the only real chance this team has to overcome the shaky pitching. The Cardinals must score runs in clusters, and be capable of doing so quickly, and the best way to do that is via the homer.

**— Columnist Bernie Miklasz, after the Cards hit seven homers July 1-2**

**108**

For the third time in their careers and first time ever at a home game, the Cardinals MV3 of Albert Pujols, Scott Rolen and Jim Edmonds each crushed home runs.

The burst of offense made any late-inning ingenuity unnecessary. No need for signs that could be mistaken for an order to lay down an 0-2 squeeze. Just the hammers at the heart of the order.

The MV3 drove in six of the Cardinals' runs in the 9-7 victory, had five of the Cardinals' 11 hits and scored five runs.

On the day he was announced as the leading vote-getter for the All-Star Game, Pujols hit a three-run blast in the third. Rolen led off the fifth by mashing his home run 446 feet to left center field — the longest home run by a Cardinal at the new ballpark. The next batter, Edmonds, followed with a solo shot that went 431 feet.

"Without question, I haven't hit a ball like that that you guys have seen at all," Rolen said. "On the road. At home. Anywhere. In batting practice. At spring training." ■

**— Post-Dispatch coverage of July 2 Cardinals-Royals game**

Scott Rolen throws from his knees in an attempt to nail Kansas City's David DeJesus, who beats the throw.

**RIGHT:** Big Mac Land at new Busch Stadium opens during a June 30 game between the Cardinals and the Kansas City Royals .

Hitting coach Hal McRae and Scott Spiezio look over the scouting report on Royals reliever Joel Peralta, and Spiezio responds with a solo homer.

Lewis, a 4-year-old bald eagle from the World Bird Sanctuary, lands near home plate as part of a pregame show July 2.

## SCOTT ROLEN   By Bernie Miklasz

Scott Rolen was all but erased from the baseball map last season. He endured two shoulder operations, a powerless .235 batting average and a summer of pain and doubt. He put his left shoulder in a sling and his career on hold. The Gold Glove was shipped to another address.

In Rolen's absence, a superbly talented new generation of third basemen began sprouting around the National League — David Wright in New York, Garrett Atkins in Colorado, Ryan Zimmerman in Washington and Cincinnati's Edwin Encarnacion. Other, more experienced third basemen moved up in prominence, including Houston's Morgan Ensberg and Chicago's Aramis Ramirez. After last season, the all-star cast became more crowded when Florida relocated the dynamic Miguel Cabrera from left field to third.

Rolen, the forgotten man, went away to heal for the winter.

A physical rehabilitation was just one part of the comeback.

Much of Rolen's trauma was emotional and psychological.

"My first fear was that I may never play again," Rolen said. "The doctors said that fear was probably unwarranted, but I'm not a doctor. If you go in for a heart surgery, a heart surgeon probably looks at it a little differently than the patient would look at the surgery. A small procedure to a heart surgeon is an enormous procedure to you and I. It's not something you mess around with.

"So my first question was, 'What if I can't play anymore?' When I was playing last year— if you want to call it 'playing' — I couldn't do anything. And now I have the second surgery, and after the post-op and the way you feel, the lack of strength and range of motion and everything — I worried I may never play again. And the second fear was, 'How bad will I be?' If I do play, when is this thing going to respond? Is it going to respond? Am I going to be stronger, and am I going to be better — or am I going to be weaker, am I going to be worse?"

After two shoulder surgeries, Scott Rolen picks up where he left off as an elite third baseman.

Rolen goes all out to make it home safely on a single and three-base error against the Cubs.

Rolen provided firm, unequivocal answers the first half of the season. He entered July as one of the National League's leading hitters and was named to the All-Star team for the fifth consecutive season. Rolen's fielding at third base is not only at the usual gold level; he may qualify for platinum.

And those fabulous NL third basemen may not be aware of Rolen's comeback. Rolen is no showboat, so there will be no declarations about his intention to reclaim his lost prestige. But Rolen, the old-school type, is making the best kind of statement through a reassuring performance.

"If any of those other guys can play the position 15 years and get to the Hall of Fame, they're in Scott Rolen's class," Cardinals manager Tony La Russa said. "They may get there. Maybe not. But Scott Rolen can get to the Hall of Fame. He's the standard."

Rolen knows much of the season is ahead of him. The rebuilt left shoulder must last. He must avoid other injuries. He can't wear down. But he's come a great distance in a relatively short time. It wasn't long ago that Rolen dreaded surgery for reasons that had nothing to do with baseball — and everything to do with being a husband to Niki and a father to their daughter, Raine Tyler.

Raine was born on Jan. 5, 2005. And as Rolen was prepped for shoulder surgery

Scott Rolen connects for the game-winning hit July 15 against the Dodgers.

In the heat of the pennant race, Rolen unloads on umpire Tim Tschida. "We had a disagreement about the strike zone before, during and after that at-bat," says Rolen, who gets ejected.

on May 13, 2005, and then again on July 25, his head and heart were overloaded with heavy thoughts.

"I'm not a big fan of looking at things through a baseball perspective necessarily," Rolen said. "I have a wife and daughter. And I'm getting put out under general anesthesia — twice. Sure, it's my job, it's my career, I have to go through the surgeries. I understand that and I have no problem with that.

"Before you have a child, you don't think much about it. Just 'Knock me out. We'll see what happens.' I always have a bad reaction to the anesthesia. So if I get sick a little and have some double vision, I'll be fine. But all of a sudden, my daughter is in the equation. And I'm thinking, 'I need to wake up from this.' I'm not worried about the surgery. But the anesthetics were troubling. That was more of a life thing than a baseball thing. And to have to do it twice last summer was disturbing. That was the fear for me, that I wouldn't wake up."

That was Rolen's low ebb. His hopes were restored last winter, on his first practice swing since the surgery. Rolen set up a batting tee and a net in his home garage. He put a baseball on the tee. And he punished it. He had a better swing, right there, than he put on a baseball during all of 2005.

It was Rolen's reawakening, in more ways than one.

Scott Rolen goes airborne, but even his Gold Glove can't get to every line drive.

Rolen and So Taguchi get their game faces on as David Eckstein springs out of the dugout for a first-inning at-bat.

# Fast-break offense

**July 13-16, 2006**

I t took 14 innings for a game that began most frustratingly to end most predictably on its 424th pitch. Given a whack at his personal pinata, Albert Pujols provided the Cardinals a sudden victory over the Los Angeles Dodgers when he drove a one-out home run off lefthander Odalis Perez for a 3-2 win.

El Hombre paused to savor his 421-foot drive as it bored into the left field seats. He then rounded the bases, tapped home plate and made a playful sprint away from teammates waiting to pound him for ending a game that lasted 4 hours, 21 minutes.

The blast left Pujols with 10 hits, five home runs and 12 RBIs in 15 career at-bats against Perez.

"That's why people pay attention to numbers," manager Tony La Russa said. "There's obviously a confidence factor there with Albert. It wasn't like he gave him an easy at-bat."

Albert Pujols blasts a walk-off home run in the bottom of the 14th to beat the Dodgers.

"Any time you hit a walk-off home run, that's the best home run in the game," Pujols said. "I'm just glad we're not playing (anymore). A long game like this, the first game after the (All-Star) break, you battle through it." ■

**— Post-Dispatch coverage of July 13 Cardinals-Dodgers game.**

## MOMENTS

"We went through something like this in 2001 and came out OK. There's no reason for anyone to be negative. We're in first place, it's July, and we haven't played our best ball yet. This is a great team. It's what I believe, even if people want to pick us apart."

**— Albert Pujols, on coming out of the All-Star break with 20 losses in 34 games**

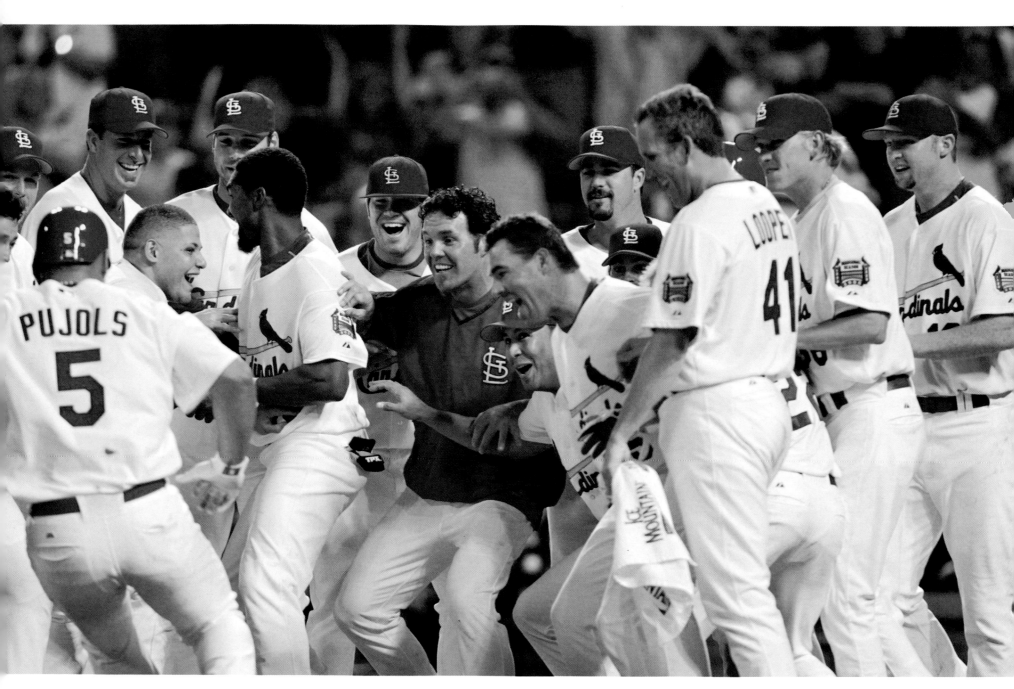

Albert Pujols takes a playful left turn as if to avoid the home-plate mob in the 14th inning. By the time he gets home, Pujols is able to edge a toe onto the plate.

## MOMENTS

"He's had a great start so far. And he seems to like being around his dad, and all the knowledge his dad's got, it's got to be helping Chris. He's not afraid to ask questions. It's going to be a big positive on his side in the long run to be able to go out there and accept all the knowledge he can get. He wants to learn, and that's the most impressive thing to me."

**— Jim Edmonds,
on rookie Chris Duncan**

Rookie Chris Duncan brings stability to the lineup and a welcome jolt of power to the Cardinals.

Chris Carpenter earns a pat on the chest from pitching coach Dave Duncan after throwing a two-hit shutout against the Dodgers. For the stoic Duncan, that's about as effusive as the postgame celebrations get.

## MOMENTS

As we continue to pull our hair, clutch our shirts and hope our weak and exasperated hearts don't come bursting out of our chests like some alien invader every time we watch the Cardinals play a hard nine, it's now quite obvious how Cardinal Nation will be spending the rest of its long summer days.

Hold on to your anxieties, fluff up your insecurities and embrace your frazzled nerves. Slap a little Chapstick on that slightly irritated lower lip you've been gnawing on.  What you've been seeing for the last three uneasy slump-filled weeks  is exactly how it's going to be for the rest of the Redbirds' season.

This is a team full of big boppers, adventurous fielders, schizoid starting pitchers and a bullpen full of adrenaline junkies. That is a wicked combination for the faint of heart who prefer games to have neat and predictable conclusions.

— Columnist Bryan Burwell,
at the All-Star break

Summer's dog days inspire attempts to stay cool. **FACING:** Umpire Chris Guccione tries the traditional cup of water to the neck. **ABOVE:** At a St. Louis Fire Department cooling station, Courtney Neisler (left) of Florissant, Mo., hops through puddles ahead of her brother, Connor Bond.

# A mighty wind

**July 17-19, 2006**

## MOMENTS

There were no tornadoes at Busch — just mighty wind, rearranging pieces of the stadium that weren't bolted down. And a hard rain that hit the skin like the sting of a bee. And there was a frightening touch of science fiction: a huge ball of dust and dirt and particles, forming and floating outside the stadium, then attacking customers inside the walls.

It was as if a vacuum cleaner sucked up all the debris from the pit where the old Busch Stadium once stood, then released it on the unsuspecting crowd.

One minute, there was sunshine. A few minutes later, there was a darkness on the edge of town.

**— Columnist Bernie Miklasz**

After two nights of the team's pitching staff being battered and two hours of the team's new ballpark being whipped and ripped by high wind, Chris Carpenter showed just how to keep an offensive gust down.

Minutes before the first pitch, a tempest of dust — presumably whipped up from a nearby construction lot — engulfed the Cardinals' new ballpark. From the upper deck of the ballpark it appeared as if dark clouds had swallowed half the Gateway Arch.

High wind hit the ballpark first, scattering fans and then loose trash, loose paper and many things that were only slightly loose. Like the plastic sheeting that's meant to shield the open-air press box from testy weather. Sheets were torn from moorings and blown into and out of the press box. Torrents of rain followed.

Fans brave gusting winds that shot through the portals between the stands and the concourse.

The grounds crew fought the wind to cover the infield even as the wind ripped a gash into the tarp. It sat on the field through most of the 2 hours 12 minutes of rain delay. Diligent workers labored to rid the center field warning track of standing water. Ankle-deep water drained from the dugouts. Home plate, flooded in the flash storm, was tidied up.

Carpenter went to work once the violent weather passed. He had a champ's reaction to the adversity and delay, holding the Braves to two runs in seven innings. ∎

**— Post-Dispatch coverage of July 19 Cardinals-Braves game**

Stadium employee Elmer Forrester tries to clear a clogged drain in the stairwell between the Cardinals Club and the seats behind home plate.

The storm whips up so quickly before the first pitch that the grounds crew really doesn't have a chance. Temporarily, at least, the wind wins the battle of the tarp.

Fans brace themselves against gusting winds that blast through Busch. "I was hanging on for dear life," usher Linda McGuire said. "The rain was hitting us so hard it felt like needles."

Infielder Aaron Miles walks through a flooded hallway between the clubhouse and the dugout .

Starting pitcher Jeff Weaver reflects on a Cardinals debut that does not go as well as planned. Weaver, acquired in a trade from the Angels, surrenders six runs in four innings on July 17.

So Taguchi does his best impersonation of Jim Edmonds but can't snag a Brian McCann drive that clears the center-field wall.

# Midseason makeover

**August 1-3, 2006**

Second baseman Ronnie Belliard and righthanded reliever Jorge Sosa, one an answer and the other a riddle, settled into a pennant race upon their arrival at Busch Stadium. Acquired by the Cardinals before the series opener against the Philadelphia Phillies, one viewed his deal as a shock, while the other may consider it a career lifeline.

Belliard moved into the Cardinals starting lineup two days after learning he was traded by the Cleveland Indians for infielder Hector Luna. Before he could think about moving from an also-ran to a contender, Belliard needed to move past the shock.

"I got surprised by the trade. I didn't hear anything about my name," said Belliard, who has never played in the postseason. "They already have the horses in here to do it. I'm just going to try and fill in. It's all about winning."

Sosa needed a new home because the Atlanta Braves designated him for assignment less than a year after he gave them 13 wins and a 2.55 ERA as a starting pitcher. He had been laboring as a closer and middle reliever before the Braves dealt him to the Cardinals for a minor league pitcher.

"It's hard to explain," Sosa said when asked the difference between 2005 and 2006. "I haven't had a good year, but I try to do my best." ∎

**— Post-Dispatch coverage of Aug. 1 Cardinals-Phillies game**

## MOMENTS

"This won't take long. No part of our team was good enough, including the manager. And I don't have anything more to say."

**— Tony La Russa, after a 16-8 loss to the Phillies**

Newly-acquired pitcher Jorge Sosa shags balls in the outfield before a game against the Phillies.

Second baseman Ronnie Belliard talks to reporters before making his Cardinals debut. Belliard says he's shocked at being traded by Cleveland for Hector Luna.

## MOMENTS

"To be able to come home and perform like that in front of my friends and family is special to me. It's one of those things you always think about, and when it happens, you hope it goes the way you want it to go."

— Lafayette High grad Ryan Howard, on hitting a homer for the Phillies in his first game in St. Louis as a major leaguer

Homecoming is sweet for St. Louisan Ryan Howard (left), the major leagues' home run leader. (Above) David Eckstein takes a bumpy ride over David Dellucci in an attempt to complete a double play.

# A rerun: 8 is enough

**August 4-6, 2006**

O n the same night the Cardinals crafted their first lead in 53 innings, a bruised division leader also produced its first win since July 26.  Not surprisingly, it was also a night when Albert Pujols stirred.

The Cardinals' sore-elbowed first baseman ended his grinding third-inning at-bat against reliever Geremi Gonzalez by driving a two-run home run for a 3-0 lead. The Cardinals went on to make a 4-0 advantage hold for a 4-3 win over the Milwaukee Brewers, breaking an eight-game losing streak and restoring a sense or normalcy to an increasingly quiet clubhouse.

"You've got to start with a success some-where, and it started tonight," manager Tony La Russa said.

Pujols' 34th home run - his first since July 25 - came after he singled, stole second and scored on third baseman Scott Rolen's first-inning double. The laser shot in the third came immediately before center fielder Jim Edmonds doubled and scored on second baseman Ronnie Belliard's single that capped a three-run inning.

The Cardinals' first win since July 26 brought an end to the team's second eight-game losing streak of the season and along with that came an unusual distinction: The Cardinals are the first team in major league history to emerge from dual eight-game losing streaks without losing first place.

Rolen's two-out, first-inning double gave the Cardinals their first lead since the first inning against the Chicago Cubs on July 29.

"Wow," Rolen replied when informed of the 53-inning drought. "Cool." ∎

**— Post-Dispatch coverage of Aug. 5 Cardinals-Brewers game**

## MOMENTS

"We don't do a whole lot of things different. I don't know how to explain it. The way I look at it is, 'What the hell are we doing wrong at night?' "

**— Tony La Russa, after the Aug. 6 victory gives the Cardinals a 29-12 daytime record, compared to 31-38 at night**

Albert Pujols is congratulated after stealing a base and scoring a first-inning run.

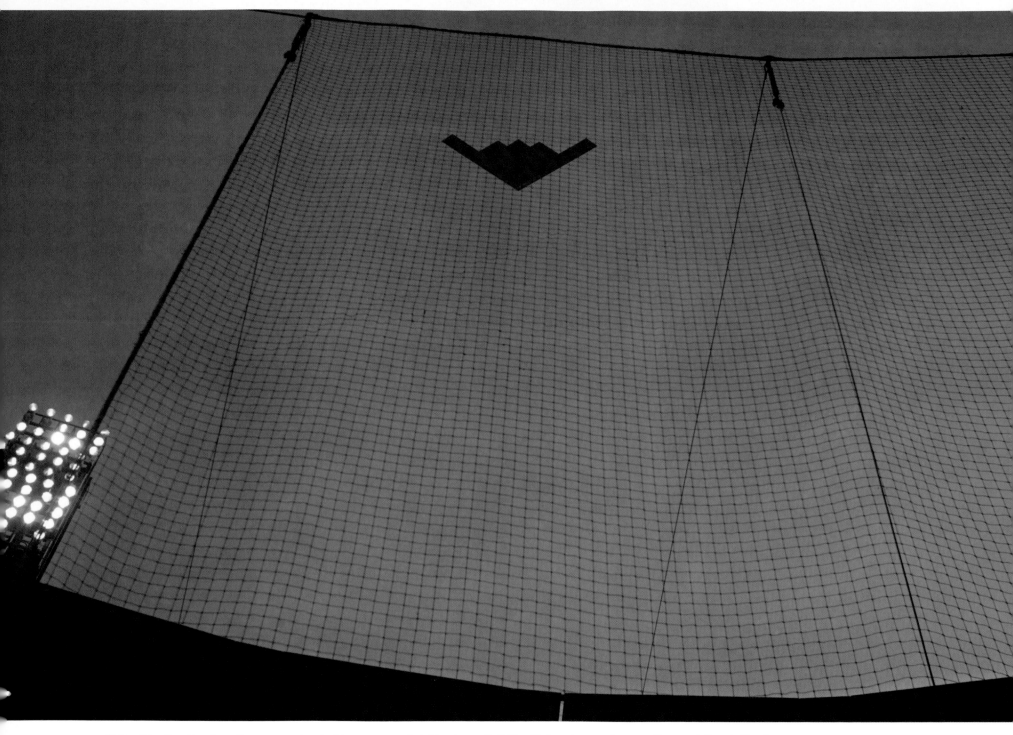

Fans attending the Aug. 5 game are treated to an unusual sight when a B-2 Stealth bomber performs a flyover at Busch Stadium.

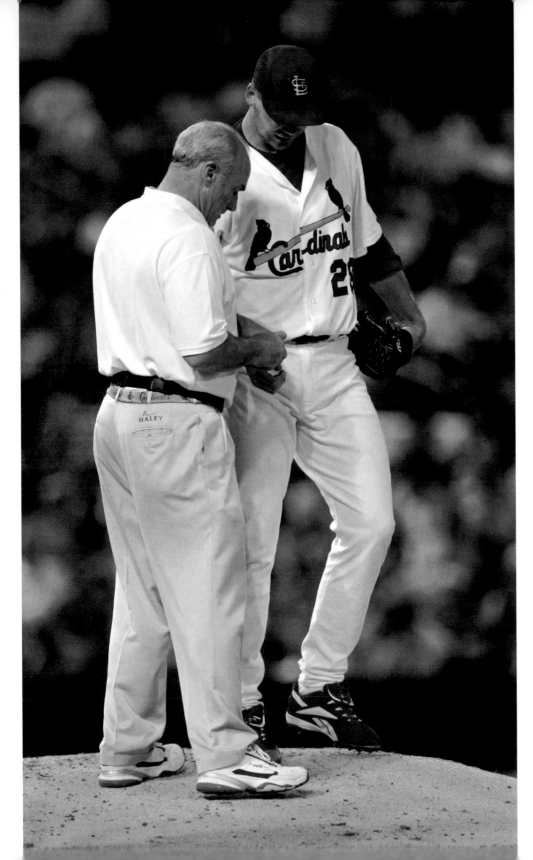

## MOMENTS

"That's a hard catch for me — the angle, the backhand, going forward. If I miss, I'm going to tear my shoulder up."

**— Center fielder Jim Edmonds, after getting the wind knocked out of him on a tumbling, game-saving catch Aug. 5**

Head trainer Barry Weinberg has a busy series, checking Chris Carpenter's hand (left) after he is hit by a one-hop smash from Bill Hall, and tending to Jim Edmonds (right) after an outfield spill.

# Let the new guys do it

**August 15-17, 2006**

On rare days like this, if Tony La Russa wants to spit in your eye and tell you it's raining, or slap an iron mallet on your noggin and swear the sky's falling, it would be wise to grab an umbrella in one hand and a hard hat in the other.

What do you say to a man who stares at a disaster, smiles and tries to convince doubters that it's an opportunity? Well, if it's La Russa gushing about his surfer-dude reclamation project, Jeff Weaver, you shake your head and call him a prophet, because in 10 days, Weaver has transformed himself from the cursed to the toast of the town.

— Bryan Burwell,
after Jeff Weaver pitches
the Cards to victory Aug. 17

**142**

For several weeks, Cardinals manager Tony La Russa has been quick to draw a distinction between this summer's team, stumbles and streaks and all, and the 100-win colossuses of the previous two seasons.

Past is past, he's said.

It's fitting, then, that three players who have no tie to the swaggering days of yore — two rookies who elbowed their way into contributing roles on this team and a castoff pitcher — would play prominently in what was a pivotal game for the present.

Against the encroaching Cincinnati Reds, Scott Rolen homered to tie the score in the seventh and singled in rookie Chris Duncan in the ninth for a 2-1 victory. Duncan had three hits as the Cardinals won the three-game series and left Busch Stadium with a 2 1/2-game lead in the division. Rookie reliever Adam Wainwright got two critical outs, and starter Jeff Weaver had his best game since being cast to the Cardinals.

Jeff Weaver's strong performance against the Reds raises hopes that the rotation has found some stability.

"This was a game that could have gone either way," La Russa said. "The way we won it is different than the way we won the first game of this series (Chris Carpenter's dominance). Not only did we have to tie them, we had to avoid the big rally in the eighth inning. This is a tough win. I think you pick up an extra plus.

"But, the question is, where does it take you?" ∎

— Post-Dispatch coverage of Aug. 17 Cardinals-Reds game

Chris Duncan can't wait for his next at bat against the Reds. Duncan goes 9 for 13 in the series, prompting Cincinnati manager Jerry Narron to say: "We can't get Chris Duncan out."

## MOMENTS

"He's a warrior. It's a big game in a big series. He did his best, like every time he takes the ball."

**— Albert Pujols, after Chris Carpenter's shutout victory Aug. 15**

**144**

Tony La Russa embraces Chris Carpenter after his 11th career shutout. The performance is about as tidy as they come: Carpenter strikes out six Reds, allows only one baserunner into scoring position and none to third base.

# An unlikely hero

**August 25-27, 2006**

The trek for catcher Gary Bennett began in Martinsville, Va., in 1990 and has continued to Batavia, Clearwater, Reading, Scranton-Wilkes Barre, Philadelphia, Pawtucket, New York, Norfolk, Denver, San Diego, Milwaukee and Washington, with a couple more stops at Scranton-Wilkes Barre mixed in.

His goal, his first major-league postseason playoff berth, hasn't been reached yet. But the Cardinals' backup catcher helped give his club and himself a giant shove in that direction this weekend.

In unquestionably the best three days of his baseball life, Bennett — replacing an injured Yadier Molina — capped a seven-for-10 series with a two-out grand slam in the ninth inning to provide a 10-6 victory over the Chicago Cubs.

Bennett had won Saturday's game with a ninth-inning single. But if Saturday was good for Bennett, Sunday was grand. After the Cardinals' first 12 hits of the game had been singles, Bennett cracked the first four-run homer of his big-league career.

"Running the bases, there's absolutely nothing going through your head," he said. "Then, when you round third and start heading home and you see all your teammates there and everybody's fired up and the crowd's going wild. ... It's 4 years old on Christmas morning. That's the feeling.

"It's awesome. I don't know how you can top it other than the World Series." ∎

**— Post-Dispatch coverage of Aug. 27 Cardinals-Cubs game**

Gary Bennett's heroics on Saturday afternoon are special ...

... but his walk-off blast to beat the Cubs in a nationally televised game Sunday night is simply grand.

Students of the game: Cardinals pitching coach Dave Duncan (left) sits with his son, outfielder Chris Duncan, in the dugout during a game against the Cubs.

Ronnie Belliard yells after being hit by a pitch from Chicago's Juan Mateo.

# A shot in the arm

**August 29-31, 2006**

## MOMENTS

"I don't want any more distractions. And that's the manager sending a message.

"... Human nature says somebody is going to be distracted (by injury questions from the media), and we cannot afford to be distracted. The race is as close as it is, and you can count on the caliber of the competition. Concentrate on the guys who are playing, not the guys who are missing."

**— Tony La Russa, announcing a new pregame-interview guideline: He would only talk about players who are playing — not those sidelined**

First-year Florida manager Joe Girardi flinched. Rather than push his signature lefthanded starter, he sided with middling righthanded relief. The Cardinals jumped at the move. Checked for seven innings by Marlins ace Dontrelle Willis, the Cardinals attacked former Chicago Cubs reliever Sergio Mitre for a four-run eighth inning that transformed a 2-1 deficit into a 5-2 win.

Stoked by Chris Duncan's score-tying pinch home run and third baseman Scott Rolen's game-winning single, the outcome was enough to invigorate manager Tony La Russa.

After watching Cardinals starting pitcher Jeff Suppan match Willis pitch for pitch, La Russa was in no mood to concede anything to anybody.

"Willis was outstanding, but I liked our approach. The way I look at it: bring on the lefthanders," La Russa said. "We've got a great chance to get them."

Suppan took a no decision in a performance that dropped his second-half ERA to 2.38 in nine starts. "We have a different team than we've had in the past," Suppan said. "From what we've had to deal with, to look at being five games up and 10 games over .500 is saying something." ■

**— Post-Dispatch coverage of Aug. 31 Cardinals-Marlins game**

Dontrelle Willis keeps the Cardinals in check — something the Florida bullpen could not do.

Ron Head, 65, of Benton, Ill., sings the national anthem before a game between the Cardinals and the Florida Marlins.

## MOMENTS

"I'm more concerned about getting this right and getting it fixed and getting back to being normal.

"I'm not going to sit here and worry about losing money. I'm not losing anything. I'm losing competing out there on the field. And that's harder than anything else."

**— Pending free agent Mark Mulder, on his season-ending shoulder surgery**

Adam Wainwright (left) emerges as a central figure in relief. The Cardinals bullpen is especially taxed because of the arm woes of Mark Mulder (right), who fails to make it out of the second inning against the Marlins.

# Special delivery

September 1-3, 2006

Each year on "Buddy Walk" day, Albert Pujols mingles with the children who are the special guests at the ballpark, fielding personal requests for a home run with a grin, a wink or a nod. There are many wishes for heroics, too many for even an MVP to satisfy.

Yet, each year, he does.

A promise fulfilled with each swing, Pujols marked Down Syndrome Awareness Day with three home runs as the Cardinals capped what could be remembered as the pivotal home stand of the season. Pujols tied a career high with the three homers and drove in five runs in the Cardinals' 6-3 victory over Pittsburgh at Busch Stadium.

The father of a daughter with Down syndrome, Pujols has hit home runs on three of the past five "Buddy Walk in the Park" days. Sunday was the sixth annual, and he has 11 RBIs in the six games played when children with Down syndrome participate in pregame ceremonies.

"He always has extra inspiration on a day like today," manager Tony La Russa said. "He's amazing. I think when we have this special day with the kids it inspires him. He's better than ever on days like this." ∎

— Post-Dispatch coverage of Sept. 3 Cardinals-Pirates game

## MOMENTS

"It's always good to do something special for those kids. Once in awhile the kids will say, 'Hit a home run for me.' It's a special day for those kids, me and my daughter, my family."

— Albert Pujols, whose daughter Isabella has Down syndrome

Albert Pujols stands with Brendan Hodges, who is announced as the "starting" first baseman on Down Syndrome Awareness Day.

Kelby Burns, of Sparta, Ill., (left) lets his second-grade classmate, Graham Nitzsche, of Evansville, Ill., try on his hat. Graham has a group of 117 friends, classmates and family at the game to support him as part of the Down Syndrome Association's "Buddy Walk" before the game. At right is Graham's sister, Sabrie Nitzsche.

Albert Pujols belts his third home run of the game, then makes a Busch Stadium curtain call.

## MOMENTS

"I hung it, and he banged it. I thought it was going to hit the St. Louis Arch out there. I wanted to go high-five him. That's unreal. That's like Superman playing baseball."

**— Pirates pitcher Ian Snell, on Albert Pujols hitting his third homer of the game off Snell — this one 447 feet**

157

## CHRIS CARPENTER  Post-Dispatch

When Chris Carpenter starts a game for the Cardinals, they have almost a three-in-four chance of winning that game. Ponder that in this age of National League parity-mediocrity (choose one), where every team but a couple seems to be a .500 club.

Carpenter made his 87th career start for the Cardinals on Sept. 1 at Busch Stadium. His 3-1 victory over Pittsburgh in a spiffy 1 hour and 54 minutes was the Cardinals' 63rd in those 87 games for a club winning percentage of .724. Carpenter himself improved to 49-16 (.754) as a Cardinal.

All this is a prelude to a not-so-premature discussion of the National League Cy Young Award, the 2005 version of which is displayed somewhere in Carpenter's New Hampshire home.

Asked whether Carpenter should win again, Cardinals manager Tony La Russa said, "Absolutely. His numbers compare to anybody."

Pitching coach Dave Duncan concurred. "Who are you going to compare him to?" asked Duncan. "Nobody's run away with a bunch of wins this year.

"He was a dominant pitcher again tonight."

Carpenter said, "That's nice of them to say. Let's win the division first, go to the playoffs and then when we get home again, we'll see what happens."

Shortstop Aaron Miles helped Carpenter out of a

Pitching coach Dave Duncan checks in on Chris Carpenter during a July 14 game against the Dodgers. Not that Carpenter needs advice — he finishes the night with a two-hit shutout.

one-on, one-out spot when he sprawled to his right for a grounder and, from his knees, threw to second for a forceout.

"As an infielder," Miles said, "you don't want to give them any freebies when he's pitching like that.

"I think he's the best I've seen from facing him and playing behind him. As far as stuff goes, there's not a tougher at-bat in the league. And from playing behind him, you know it's there every

Nobody was tougher on National League hitters than Chris Carpenter in 2006. He allowed only 1.07 baserunners per inning, the best figure in the league.

day, every time he starts."

After watching the Sept. 1 game in which Carpenter struck out eight, allowed just three singles and walked no one for the fifth time in six starts, Post-Dispatch columnist Bernie Miklasz wrote:

"May I suggest that Chris Carpenter is the closest thing we've seen to Bob Gibson among Cardinals starters that followed Gibson?

"John Tudor, Joaquin Andujar, Bob Forsch, Matt Morris, Darryl Kile and Woody Williams all had some great moments and individual seasons. But none was as dominant as Carpenter over a three-year stretch.

"Since this is only Carpenter's third season in uniform with the Cardinals, he hasn't built up the seniority needed to qualify for a list of, say, the top five starters in franchise history. Carpenter needs to pitch at a top level for a few additional seasons before he's slotted in an elite post-1900 group that includes Gibson, Dizzy Dean, Mort Cooper, Jessie "Pop" Haines, Harry "The Cat" Brecheen, Grover Cleveland Alexander, Bill Sherdel, Steve Carlton, Forsch and Morris.

"But over a three-year period, Carpenter is right there."

La Russa put it simply: "There isn't anybody in baseball who's a better pitcher than Chris Carpenter."

One of the rare times the Cardinals ace can't save face at Busch: Sam Carpenter gives dad a playful slap during the Fathers / Kids game on Father's Day.

Carpenter gets a pat on the head from catcher Yadier Molina after a four-hit, no-walk shutout of the Reds on Aug. 15.

**RIGHT:** Chris Carpenter salutes the crowd before throwing out the ceremonial first pitch at the home opener on April 10.

**FAR RIGHT:** Cardinals fans acknowledge their ace. Carpenter (foreground) gets a standing ovation as he bats in the bottom of the eighth inning, on his way to a two-hit shutout of the Dodgers on July 14.

# Back on track

**September 11-13, 2006**

After staggering through two poorly played series at Washington and Arizona, the Cardinals returned to Busch Stadium to quell a minor uprising by the Houston Astros. But this Houston surge has failed to inspire widespread panic on the streets of St. Louis.

Maybe that's because Cardinals fans feel more secure about the standings after watching ace Chris Carpenter take a chainsaw to Houston's bats. In a commanding 7-0 victory, Carpenter mastered a six-hit shutout and erased residue left from the team's uninspiring 2-5 road trip.

Carpenter's huge night stabilized the Cardinals and immobilized the Astros. When in doubt, give the rock to Carpenter.

"That's the way he pitches," manager Tony La Russa said. "He's such a horse. These guys (the Astros) are fired up to face him. But he's hitting corner after corner with a bunch of pitches. Movement on everything. He's a horse."

Shortstop Aaron Miles makes like Ozzie Smith in turning a double play to help Chris Carpenter shut out the Astros on Sept. 11

Second baseman Ronnie Belliard broke open the game with a three-run triple, but afterward could only talk about Carpenter. "He's been unbelievable," Belliard said. "He works hard. He works quick. We just play good defense behind him." ■

**— Post-Dispatch coverage of Sept. 11 Cardinals-Astros game**

## MOMENTS

"We had a disagreement with the strike zone before, during, and after it. I got the short end of it. I got thrown out of the game. That's not what I was trying to do."

**— Scott Rolen, on his heated exchange — and near contact — with umpire Tim Tschida on Sept. 12**

Umpire Tim Tschida ejects Scott Rolen for arguing after being called out on strikes Sept. 12.

## MOMENTS

"It's frustrating any way you slice it. When you make a good pitch inside and you break a guy's bat, you hope for a better result than a game-winning double."

— **Astros reliever Brad Lidge, after blowing a save by allowing the game-winning hit to Albert Pujols on Sept. 12**

Houston closer Brad Lidge and catcher Brad Ausmus have to like their chances when Albert Pujols comes to the plate in the bottom of the ninth on Sept. 12. Sure, they remember what Pujols did to them in the 2005 playoffs, but the Cardinals slugger is batting only .100 against Lidge in the regular season.

Pujols doesn't need a homer against Lidge this time around. A two-run double in the bottom of the ninth is enough to carry the Cardinals to victory.

# Rested and rollin'

**September 15-17, 2006**

## MOMENTS

Already down by four runs and batting with a couple of runners on base, Matt Morris was eager to get his at-bat going, but his former teammates would not let the moment pass unappreciated.

Pitcher Chris Carpenter stepped off the mound, and catcher Yadier Molina let Morris know that no pitch was coming, so the Busch Stadium crowd could applaud Morris' first appearance in St. Louis in a jersey other than the Cardinals'.

"I was just trying to focus on getting us back in the game, and it's hard to enjoy those when you're playing," Morris said. "It was a classy act."

**— Post-Dispatch coverage of Sept. 16 game**

For a clue that Scott Rolen's power was about to be restored and he was going to jolt spectacularly from his September slump, one had only to watch him bound and bash through Friday's batting practice.

Or one could live in Rolen's neighborhood.

Given the tonic of a day off, Rolen used it to rest his sore shoulder, calm his aching wrist, mentally recalibrate and take some needed swings out on the driveway. As if there is any place better to revive a swing than "taking dry hacks on the driveway," he said.

Rejuvenated by the homework and the off day, Rolen led an offensive bludgeoning by hitting two homers and driving in a career-best seven runs in the Cardinals' 14-4 thumping of San Francisco.

The Gold Glove third baseman is about a year removed from having his shoulder rebuilt, a joint that he said won't be at full strength until 2007's spring training. In the past week, he has dealt with the soreness in his shoulder and previously undisclosed pain in his wrist.

"Every month that I've played this year is new ground from the shoulder surgery I had last year," Rolen said. "This one didn't start off too well. Hopefully, it picks up. Got a day off, got a good day at the plate. Mentally it was a break, a chance to think about (the swing) — where it has been, where it needs to be." ∎

**— Post-Dispatch coverage of Sept. 15 Cardinals-Giants game**

Former Cardinal Matt Morris returns to St. Louis sporting a different uniform.

Scott Rolen races around first base on a bases-loaded double that drove in Chris Duncan (right) and two other runners. He has a seven-RBI game on the same day the Post-Dispatch publishes the headline, "Rolen continues to battle slump."

## MOMENTS

"It's so special to be remembered in your home park. These fans are the best. They're baseball fans here, and they do the job of passing it down from generation to generation. It means a lot to me that a dad can bring his little boy or a grandfather can bring his grandson out and there will be little kids saying, 'Tell me about those numbers. Who is that guy?'

"Every baseball player wants to be remembered, whether it's for a pitch or a play or a season or something like that. To be up there for all time in a stadium like this ... kind of gives you immortality as a baseball player. You keep getting better and better over the years."

**— Bruce Sutter, as his No. 42 is retired and his likeness displayed on the left-field wall**

"Sign Man" Marty Prather of Springfield, Mo., brings along some props so that he can deliver a message to San Francisco slugger Barry Bonds.

Bruce Sutter's No. 42 jersey is unveiled at a ceremony retiring his number from the Cardinals. It can be seen on the left-field wall. Throughout the year, the new stadium is updated with tributes to Cardinals tradition.

# Healing with one swing

**September 25-27, 2006**

**A**s this horrific late-September slump raged, desperate Cardinals fans sought alternative therapies to heal their ailing team. On Internet message boards, the calls went out for prayers, hexes, lucky charms, the ritual burning of sage. Anything to reverse the hideously evil karma that seemed to permeate Busch Stadium.

None of this would be necessary. With the stadium clock ticking toward 10 p.m., the solution and the cure would be provided by a familiar figure, a calming influence, the game's best hitter, a St. Louis icon, the Musial for younger generations of Cardinals fans.

His name, of course, is Albert Pujols. We call him El Hombre.

And all the Cardinals needed was a mighty, perfect swing from Pujols to restore their breathing, restore their pulse rate, restore their universe.

With the San Diego Padres four outs from completing a three-game series sweep that would shove the Cardinals deeper into depression and misery, Pujols chased the blues away and turned the power back on. With 40,358 standing and hoping and pleading, Pujols connected cleanly and with violent intent. He walloped a three-run shot high into the night, giving the Cardinals a 4-2 victory and oxygen.

Few Pujols bombs could match the impact of this one. The home run wiped out a 2-1 deficit and shattered the Cardinals' brutal seven-game losing streak. The home run filled the stadium with laughter and life. It generated a needed burst of joy in the home-team dugout and clubhouse. It made an increasingly bleak situation seem less ominous. ■

— **Post-Dispatch coverage of Sept. 27 Cardinals-Padres game**

## MOMENTS

"I might make that pitch 100 times a year and get away with it. Not tonight. He's Albert Pujols. What more can you say?"

— **Padres reliever Cla Meredith, on giving up the game-winning homer to Albert Pujols**

Donna Evers of O'Fallon, Mo., stays in her seat long after the stadium has emptied following a loss to the Padres.

Albert Pujols hugs teammate Ronnie Belliard after hitting a three-run homer in the eighth inning in the final game of the series with San Diego. The blast snaps a seven-game losing streak and helps the Cardinals cling to first.

## MOMENTS

"I think Encarnacion hit me in the head pretty hard. I think he's trying to keep me out of the lineup. I don't know if he wants to keep playing center field or what."

— **Jim Edmonds,
already suffering from
post-concussion syndrome,
on the team's rowdy
celebration of his three-run
pinch homer Sept. 25**

Jim Edmonds watches his pinch-hit home run tie the series opener against San Diego. It's the first at-bat in a month for Edmonds, who is suffering from post-concussion syndrome. But the dramatic homer is not enough to lift the Cardinals out of their tailspin.

Edmonds' return brings smiles to the Cardinals dugout. "Whatever room there is for me, I'll do whatever it takes," he says.
"We've got to find a way to win or it's going to get pretty ugly pretty quick."

# A sigh of relief

**September 28-October 1, 2006**

Saturday afternoon, the sky over Busch Stadium was intermittent, much like the home team on the field below. The sunshine gave way to clouds, and the brightness was dimmed to gray. Milwaukee's hard-throwing Ben Sheets put a chill through the ballpark by escaping several jams when the Cardinals threatened.

Jeff Cirillo pinch-hit for Sheets in the seventh and delivered a two-run single off Jeff Suppan, and a scoreless game was cracked open, 2-0, by the Brewers. Busch was hushed. With two outs and the bases loaded in the eighth, Scott Spiezio was dispatched to pinch-hit against Milwaukee's intimidating closer, Francisco Cordero.

Spiezio narrowly avoided dismissal on a close, two-strike pitch that didn't quite fit home plate umpire Tim Timmons' erratic strike zone. Ball one. Spiezio exhaled. Whew.

On a 1-2 count, Cordero threw a sizzling fastball, and Spiezio scorched a triple into the right-field corner. And now the Cardinals were finally getting somewhere, with all three runners scoring for a 3-2 lead.

Rookie reliever Adam Wainwright closed down the Brewers in a scoreless ninth, and the Cardinals reduced their magic number for clinching the National League Central to one.

"It's as big a hit as we've had all year," manager Tony La Russa said.  ■

**— Post-Dispatch coverage of Cardinals-Brewers game Sept. 30**

## MOMENTS

"I'm not a guy to complain when I'm not in the lineup. I know when there's a chance to be used later in the game and that one hit might be more valuable than four at-bats. And today was a perfect example."

**— Scott Spiezio, after his bases-loaded triple beat the Brewers on Sept. 30**

The "Imperial" is Scott Spiezio's way of wearing his Cardinals pride on his chin. Cards fans call it the "Spiezio."

Pinch-hitter Scott Spiezio delivers a bases-loaded triple for the game-winning hit in the eighth inning against Milwaukee on Sept. 30. Spiezio's hit helps reduce the Cardinals' magic number to one.

## MOMENTS

The division officially became theirs at 2:41 p.m. as Juan Encarnacion drove a fly ball to left field for the first out of the fifth inning. As Ronnie Belliard approached the plate, the stadium sound system pulsed with the Atlanta Braves' signature Tomahawk Chop. The score was final: Braves 3, Astros 1.

Brewers pitcher Carlos Villanueva stepped from the mound and Belliard from the batter's box as the stadium matrix proclaimed the division title. Plate umpire Derryl Cousins motioned for the game to resume but Villanueva allowed the celebration to last a few more seconds.

"I wanted to give them their moment," Villanueva said.

**— Post-Dispatch coverage of Oct. 1 Cards-Brewers game**

**178**

Albert Pujols hops in celebration as Juan Encarnacion scores the game-winning run Sept. 30 on a bases-loaded triple by Scott Spiezio.

Tony La Russa joins Albert Pujols in saluting the Busch Stadium crowd after the final game of the season. The Cardinals lose the game, but wrap up the NL Central title when Houston loses to Atlanta earlier in the day.

# Built from spare parts

October 3-8, 2006

## MOMENTS

When Albert Pujols looked at the lineup card before Game 1 of the playoffs, he turned and walked away for a few steps, then took a second look to confirm what he'd seen:

Eckstein, Duncan, Pujols, Edmonds, Rolen, Encarnacion, Belliard, Molina, Carpenter.

"I looked at it again," Pujols said, "and I thought, 'This is a good team. This is the team we're supposed to have on the field.' And that's a good lineup, man."

— Post-Dispatch

A team built around large, expensive and at times ill-fitting pieces came together to form a functional mosaic Sunday night at Busch Stadium. Its Game 4 glue came from parts unknown, or at least places no one could have guessed six months or even six weeks ago.

Confronted with the unpleasant possibility of a Monday morning flight to play a decisive game, the Cardinals overcame a first-inning pratfall by their signature starting pitcher to secure a 6-2 win over the San Diego Padres, and with it their third National League Division Series in as many years.

The Cardinals advanced because:

• Ronnie Belliard, found for the season's first four months in Cleveland, granted the Cardinals a first-inning tie following a jarring start to the night.

Julie Boyer finds her big hand to be perfect for holding drinks and giving a high-fist during the division series.

• April's Invisible Man, Juan Encarnacion, provided the game-winning RBI on a sixth-inning triple.

• A player raised from Seattle's career dead, Scott Spiezio, gave them a two-run cushion.

• Reliever Josh Kinney, a  former River City Rascal and now a 27-year-old rookie, pulled off an eighth-inning escape.

• Adam Wainwright, a pitcher unable to make the team's April starting rotation,  found himself the obvious choice to throw the clincher's final pitch.

"Every team that wins needs guys who aren't expected to come up big in the clutch," Spiezio said. "You look at what's happened here, that's what it is." ■

— Post-Dispatch coverage of Cardinals-Padres playoff game Oct. 8

For one day at least, the Padres have the Cardinals down. David Eckstein hits the dirt to avoid a pitch by Scott Linebrink in the eighth inning of Game 3.

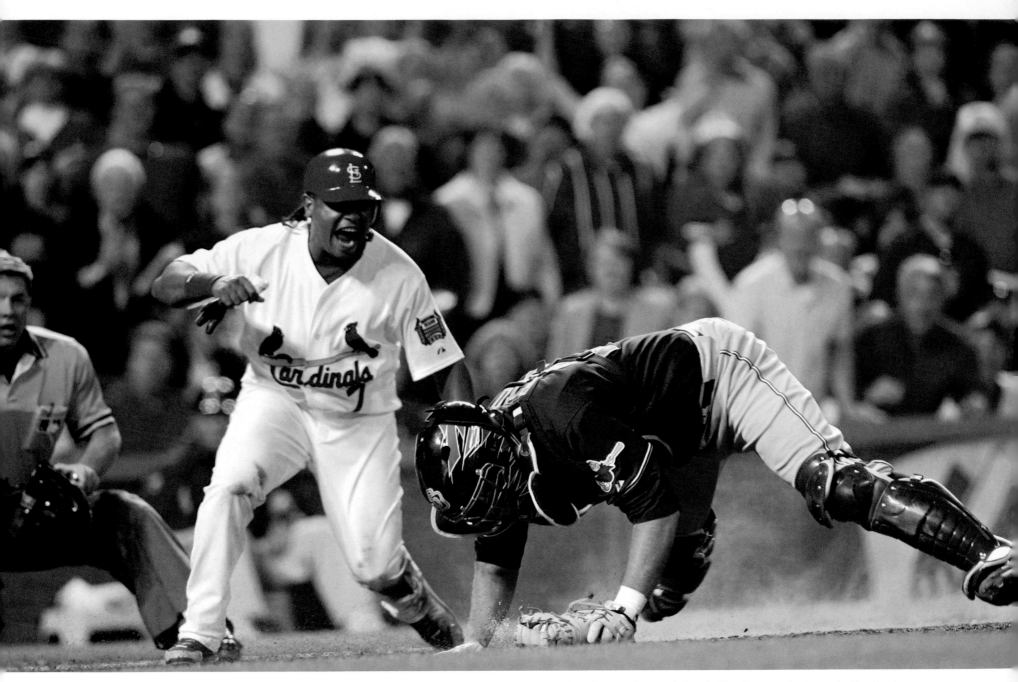

Second baseman Ronnie Belliard scores in the sixth inning of Game 4, avoiding the tag of Padres catcher Josh Bard. The four-run inning puts the Cards up 6-2 and ignites the celebration of the team's third consecutive trip to the National League Championship Series.

Rookie reliever Adam Wainwright celebrates with the crowd after closing out Game 4 against the Padres. Wainwright gets the final out for all three Cardinals victories in the series.

Albert Pujols uncorks
a champagne celebration
in the clubhouse.

# An amazin' story

**October 12-19, 2006**

**MOMENTS**

"It's fun to be an underdog for a change.

"The last couple of seasons, we were expected to win. That can be a difficult role. It might be more fun this way."

— Cardinals chairman Bill DeWitt Jr.

If red indeed once meant go for this team, then 46,496 white towels meant anything but surrender for the Cardinals at Busch Stadium. A team once mistaken for October dead continued its improbable attempt at a second World Series appearance in three years when it defeated the New York Mets 4-2 in Game 5 of the NL Championship Series. Leading the series three games to two, the Cardinals' task is brutally simple: win one of the next two at Shea Stadium and advance to face the Detroit Tigers.

"If we can't win one of the next two games we don't belong there," manager Tony La Russa said.

A day after his manager rated him a health risk, sore-legged first baseman Albert Pujols punctured Mets starter Tom Glavine's postseason aura of invincibility with a fourth-inning home run.

Sami Wielansky, 16, of Town and Country, Mo., proudly displays her "Spiezio" during Game 3 of the NLCS.

Five days after losing the same matchup in Game 1, Cards starter Jeff Weaver took the win in return for standing firm after the Mets jumped him for two fourth-inning runs and a fleeting lead.

Less than three weeks after gaining his second and third major-league saves, rookie closer pro tem Adam Wainwright converted his second of the postseason by securing the final four outs, the first with the tying run at second base in the eighth inning. ∎

— **Post-Dispatch coverage of Cardinals-Mets playoff game Oct. 17**

Tony La Russa exchanges greetings with So Taguchi before the start of Game 3 at Busch Stadium. Taguchi's ninth-inning home run off Billy Wagner in Game 2 proves to be a turning point in the series.

Cardinals fans leap from their seats as Mets right fielder Shawn Green hits the turf and misses Scott Spiezio's looping two-run triple in the first inning of Game 3.

## MOMENTS

"I swung. It ran into my bat. I don't know why that is."

**— Jeff Suppan, on becoming the first Cardinals pitcher since Bob Gibson in 1968 to hit a postseason homer**

Jeff Suppan's drive clears the glove of Mets left fielder Endy Chavez for a home run in Game 3 at Busch Stadium. "They say I don't smile in the dugout," Cards manager Tony La Russa says. "But I was smiling there. I thought we got a one-run gift."

Chris Duncan rounds the bases after delivering a pinch-hit home run in the sixth inning of Game 5. Duncan's home run gives the Cards a two-run lead and electrifies the Busch Stadium crowd.

"This is the greatest thing ever. We're going to the Series," says Dwayne Dainty of Lewiston, Ill., who reacts to the final out of Game 5 at Busch.

# This one's for all of you

BY BERNIE MIKLASZ

The 10th World Series championship in Cardinals history was for all the Cardinals teams of the past that played special baseball all summer, only to come up short, staggering off into the winter, filled with frustration and longing.

This was to give peace to all of the postseason ghosts and to soften the haunted memories, whether it's Curt Flood's slip in 1968, or umpire Don Denkinger's blown call at first base in 1985, or the hydraulic tarp that swallowed Vince Coleman's ankle.

This was for the franchise immortals who always return home, a college of Cardinals, visiting this baseball Vatican in St. Louis. They are living monuments: Stan Musial, Bob Gibson, Lou Brock, Ozzie Smith, Red Schoendienst and Bruce Sutter.

This was for old friends who could not be there, but you know that the spirits of Jack Buck and Darryl Kile were close to the Cardinals and their fans, watching over the drama of Game 5.

This was for baseball's best fans, who had waited 23 seasons for a reaffirmation of the proud franchise's glorious tradition. It doesn't matter where they were gathered for Game 5. They could have been shivering in the frigid bowl of Busch Stadium, or watching by the fireplace at home, or bonding with friends in a local sports bar, or watching on satellite from a base camp in Iraq, or an outpost in Afghanistan.

Cardinals fans live everywhere, existing as one extended family, and they became one nation under a groove again on Oct. 27, 2006, when the power of this Red October pulled their heartbeats together in an electric moment. At 10:26 on a chilly Friday night at Busch, rookie Cardinals closer Adam Wainwright struck out the Tigers' Brandon Inge on a heinous breaking ball, sealing World Series title No. 10 with a 4-2 victory in Game 5.

(Clockwise from top left) Joe Wurtz, Brian Dowdy, Cindy Parres and Jennifer Walsh arrive early for Game 5 of the World Series and claim spots outside the center-field fence at Busch Stadium.

"We shocked the world," Cardinals center fielder Jim Edmonds said on the field, moments after the game.

Their summer of lurching to 83 wins was traded in for a month of unexpected excellence. Their season of agony was exchanged for October ecstasy. Six months of adversity and trouble was washed away by champagne and bubbles in a postgame house party.

One man stood in the center of it all, nearly incapable of comprehending the magnitude of the scene. "I'm having a hard time holding it together," manager Tony La Russa said.

Jeff Weaver, the winning pitcher in Game 5, strikes out nine in his eight-inning performance.

Postseason hero Yadier Molina singles to left in Game 5. The Cardinals catcher leads the team with 19 postseason hits.

This championship was for La Russa, too. When he accepted the Cardinals job after the 1995 season, he specifically asked for No. 10. More than a number, it represented an ideal, a goal, a mission statement. The Cardinals had won the World Series nine times, and La Russa wanted to collect the 10th for the franchise.

"As soon as you put the uniform on," La Russa said, "you realize it comes with an attachment. There's a special pressure and responsibility. And that's good. It really drives you."

At times the No. 10 got awfully heavy, as the intense La Russa worked himself into a high level of stress. He'd get close, only to

be denied again, and demonized again. La Russa absorbed criticism, stirred controversy and had the name "Whitey Herzog" thrown in his face a million times.

La Russa did it his way, and whether you like him or not, this is the absolute truth: No one in a Cardinals uniform has ever worked harder or cared more deeply or lost more sleep in the quest of a World Series championship. And on Oct. 27, La Russa finally became a champ again.

"Winning a World Series is always special," La Russa said. "But we had so many opportunities here. It's been 11 years. So this is something that you really cherish."

La Russa's small office was packed. His wife, Elaine, was there; earlier they'd hugged and kissed near the Cardinals dugout only seconds after Wainwright finished what Jeff Weaver started to make 46,638 hearts skip at Busch.

An hour later, La Russa's pulse was still racing. This was his seventh postseason team in St. Louis. And who would have imagined this assortment of bruised players, slumping stars, limping veterans, precocious kids, recycled parts and superstars Albert Pujols and Chris Carpenter would rally, unify, and pull off a miracle? La Russa is only the second manager in baseball history to win a World Series in both leagues, and that distinction will guarantee his spot in Cooperstown.

In the end, these flawed but resilient Cardinals did it for superior St. Louis teams that didn't survive October. The Cardinals' postseason universe was balanced in this fantasy October.

When La Russa saw Bob Gibson after Game 5, the meaning of it all suddenly rushed through his blood.

"When you're here," La Russa said, "you can't join the club unless you win the World Series. And now we can say this group joined the club."

In his 1,851st game as the Cardinals manager, regular season and postseason, Tony La Russa got it done. The number on his back is no longer 10 pounds of burdensome weight, or the symbol of an unfulfilled promise. It stands for 10 World Series championships. An imperfect team delivered a perfect 10. ■

First baseman Albert Pujols throws to pitcher Jeff Weaver for an out on a ball hit by Detroit's Placido Polanco in Game 5.
Pujols is solid at the plate and spectacular in the field during the postseason.

## MOMENT

"Whenever David is playing, there is absolutely no doubt that our club responds to how hard he plays and how committed he is to doing whatever the team needs. He is a wonderful leader on and off the field and not just quietly. He can also be very vocal. And believe me, he's more than just guts. He's a very good player."

**— Tony La Russa, on David Eckstein**

The turning point in Game 4: Tigers left fielder Craig Monroe misses a double by David Eckstein that scores Aaron Miles with the go-ahead run in the eighth inning. Eckstein's pop surprises Monroe, who comes inches short of the catch.

David Eckstein lashes his game-winning double in Game 4. The Cardinals shortstop overcomes a slow start in the Series and finishes with eight hits in his final 11 at-bats.

The moment St. Louis has waited 24 years for: Adam Wainwright punctuates the last out and leads the championship celebration.

Center fielder Jim Edmonds and catcher Yadier Molina share a midair embrace in front of first baseman Albert Pujols. Edmonds, who misses almost all of September with post-concussion syndrome, regains his hitting stroke in the postseason.

Superstars, role players, rookies and rejects join as one team to celebrate an improbable Cardinals world championship. It's the 10th overall for the franchise and the first since 1982.

The St. Louis skyline explodes with fireworks, and the streets and stands explode with excitement after the Cardinals defeat the Tigers 4-2 in Game 5 and clinch the World Series title.

Fans in the stands, armed with special Stadium Editions of the St. Louis Post-Dispatch, wait for players to return to the field for a World Series post-game celebration.

## MOMENTS

"It's all about who's the hottest, who believes in each other and who goes out there and plays the hardest.

"And I think the struggle toward the end (of the regular season) just refreshed us once it was all done. We were able to take a deep breath, go out there and play for the second season."

— Game 5 winner Jeff Weaver

The Game 5 winning pitcher, Jeff Weaver, has tears in his eyes as he celebrates with teammate So Taguchi. Weaver, whose career is left for dead in the summer, emerges as a postseason hero in the fall.

The Cardinals brain trust — (from left) Chairman Bill DeWitt Jr., general manager Walt Jocketty and manager Tony La Russa — has ample reason to smile after Game 5.

A.J. Pujols enjoys the view from atop the shoulders of his dad, Albert Pujols, as they join the celebration after the Cardinals' Game 5 victory.

Scott Rolen lets the emotion and the bubbly pour out as he participates in the post-Game 5 party.

Outfielder Chris Duncan pours champagne on his dad, pitching coach Dave Duncan. The elder Duncan's advice is a key in the postseason. "He's like, 'This is your stuff; here it is. And this is how you're going to succeed with it,'" pitcher Chris Carpenter says.

Pitcher Jeff Suppan, the MVP of the League Championship Series, gets ready to pop the cork in the Cardinals clubhouse. Suppan gives a resilient performance to help the Cardinals win Game 4 of the World Series.

Teresa Davidson (left) and Brigid Oddy, both of St. Louis, celebrate on the streets outside Busch Stadium after the Cardinals clinch the 2006 World Series.

Cardinals catcher Yadier Molina shakes hands with a fan as Molina leaves the stadium after Game 5. Molina, always a defensive stalwart, emerges as a fan favorite during the postseason for his offensive contributions.

Cardinals manager Tony La Russa pumps his fists in time to the music as he rides with his family, including daughter Bianca (right), during the Oct. 29 parade down Market Street celebrating the Cardinals' World Series victory.

Fans along Market Street cheer for World Series MVP David Eckstein. It's a picture-perfect autumn day for a parade, with sunny skies and a temperature hitting 70.

Albert Pujols waves to the crowd during the parade. "I've been dreaming about this since I was little boy," Pujols says.

Jeff Weaver revels in the cheers from Cardinal Nation during the victory parade.

Weaver finds acceptance in St. Louis after the Angels give up on him in July and trade him to the Cardinals for a minor league outfielder.

Winless in three previous visits to the playoffs, Weaver wins a game in each round of the 2006 postseason.

Cardinals shortstop David Eckstein, the World Series MVP, acknowledges the crowd's chants of "MVP! MVP!"

Cardinals fans pour into Busch Stadium to attend the rally after the victory parade. City officials estimate that 500,000 people turn out to salute the team.

## MOMENTS

"I've been here a long time, and I think we've all shared a dream. And we can officially say that when we got that last out in Game 5, our championship dream came true.

"Let's enjoy it."

**— Tony La Russa, at the Busch Stadium celebration Oct. 29**

Manager Tony La Russa embraces his wife, Elaine (left), and daughter, Devon, at the post-parade rally in Busch Stadium. He's celebrating his second World Series title, but it's his first parade, since the 1989 festivities in Oakland were canceled in the wake of an earthquake.

Donita Tegeler (left) of Jennings, Mo., and Greg Stewart (right) of St. Louis watch the ceremony on the scoreboard during the World Series celebration rally.

Ryan Grant of University City, Mo., watches video highlights and cheers during the Oct. 29 rally. Fans receive free tickets to the rally by registering online the day before.

So Taguchi shares his World Series-winning enthusiasm with fans sitting in center field during the rally at Busch Stadium.

## MOMENTS

"We tested the patience of our great fans this year throughout the regular season. I just want to thank them for sticking with us.

"It's the ultimate feeling to be able to say that we're world champs."

— **World Series MVP David Eckstein**

THIRD BASE

3

Cardinals fans stream out of Busch Stadium past the statue of Stan Musial after the victory rally for the World Series champion St. Louis Cardinals.

# CONTENTS

All photos by **Chris Lee** of the Post-Dispatch staff, unless otherwise indicated below.

Cover photo by **J.B. Forbes**

Back photo by **Chris Lee**

Text for the inside flaps of the book cover by **Vahé Gregorian** of the Post-Dispatch.